The Unresolved Tension

Individualism or Community?

Pat Lynch

Hodder & Stoughton

LONDON SYDNEY AUCKLAND

Copyright © 1997 Pat Lynch

First published in Great Britain in 1997

The right of Pat Lynch to be identified as the Author of the Work has been asserted by him in accordance with the Copyright, Designs and Patents Act 1988.

1 3 5 7 9 10 8 6 4 2

British Library Cataloguing in Publication Data
A record for this book is available from the British Library

ISBN 0 340 64198 3

Typeset by Avon Dataset Ltd, Bidford-on-Avon, Warks

Printed in England by
Clays Ltd, St Ives plc

Hodder and Stoughton
A division of Hodder Headline PLC
338 Euston Road
London NW1 3BH

Contents

Acknowledgments

I am grateful to all those who have helped me to understand Christian community: my own family, my schools and colleges, my neighbours and especially the members of Sion Catholic Community to which I am privileged to belong.

This manuscript has gone through numerous drafts and revisions. My thanks go to Mrs Frances Landreth, my faithful secretary, and Mrs Diane Lamb, my efficient personal assistant, for making sense of my handwriting and somehow managing to put it into logical, coherent prose. Their expertise and toil have saved me hours of labour.

I am grateful to Mr Eric Major, the former Managing Director of Hodder and Stoughton, for inviting me to write this book and Mrs Elspeth Taylor for acting as my editor. Her helpful critique enabled me to clarify certain parts of the text.

Few books are the sole product of the author alone. This is certainly true in this case. My thanks to David Murray (Sion Community) for his help with Chapters 7 and 8 and to Dr David Clarke, Dr Michael Green and Rev. Russ Parker for their assistance with Chapter 6.

The library staff at Westhill College in Birmingham have been a tremendous help to me during the months of writing this book. They have afforded me space and resources which made my task so much lighter.

Thanks are due to Sion Community who were prepared to allow me to spend time researching the book and on occasion took over my workload so that I could meet deadlines.

I am grateful to those people whose work on this topic I have read.

Instead of giving extensive notes I have referred the reader to their original publications.

I acknowledge with gratitude the permission of Darton, Longman and Todd to quote from the *Jerusalem Bible*. All references, unless otherwise stated, are from the *Jerusalem Bible*.

Pat Lynch
Sion Community
June 1997

Foreword

'*Some people go to church to worship God. But I hope that's not why you're here today.*'

As the words left my lips, the congregation fell silent. Their shock was almost audible. But it's true. The reason we 'go to church' *isn't* to worship God. We can do that at home, or walking in the park, or lying in the bath, or riding on the bus. In fact, we can worship God anywhere at any time – and, of course, in absolute solitude. The real reason we 'go to church' is to worship God *together*. And it's the 'together' bit that's so important, though tragically, all too often, the reality is that even then we simply end up worshipping alone in a crowd.

When I was growing up, my parents took me to church every Sunday. One of my lasting memories is of everyone sitting sternly in their pews and facing the front, where the preacher stood dwarfed by a huge pulpit, surrounded by vases of flowers and dressed in black, looking like Darth Vadar. I also remember how, whenever I dared to sneak a quick glance round at any of the other members of the congregation, I almost invariably found my eyes met an extremely disapproving look commanding me to turn back round, face the front again and concentrate on singing the hymn or listening to the sermon. Church was for worshipping God, not for smiling at other worshippers.

I recently visited a chapel that brought all of this home to me again very vividly. The pews there were actually designed so that each seat was like a little cubicle. Unless you stood up and peered over the barriers, you couldn't even *see* your neighbour. The idea was to focus all your attention on the raised pulpit at the front of the building, the minister . . . and God. The extreme individuality of this approach, in which families couldn't even sit together as we had done in my childhood, stemmed, I suppose, from that chapel's (or at least its architect's) theology.

The Baptist tradition, in which I grew up and of which I'm now an ordained minister, has always made a point of drawing on its Reformation roots by emphasising the *personal* nature of salvation. It's one of the denomination's great strengths. But it's also one of its greatest weaknesses. As Christians from all wings of the Church have gradually discovered, stressing the importance of personal conversion can slowly push the equally important notion of community to the sidelines. The truth is, however, that being a Christian is just as much about community involvement as about personal transformation.

Finding that right balance between the individual and the community is the 'unresolved tension' that this book is all about. An individual only really comes into their own within a community. But by the same token, a community that doesn't recognise and value the individuality of its members is no community at all. As Paul says in 1 Corinthians 12:12, 'The body is a unit, though it is made up of many parts; and though all its parts are many, they form one body.'

The irony is that Christians have had a model for this unity-in-diversity, this 'unresolved tension', all along in the person of God himself. Because, as Pat Lynch points out, God is not one, but one-in-three. We give lip service to the Trinity in our creeds, but we rarely appreciate its full meaning. The three persons of God – Father, Son and Holy Spirit – make up a community. What the Council of Chalcedon (451AD) said of the humanity and divinity of Jesus is equally true of the Trinity – its persons are indivisibly distinct: 'Without confusion, without change, without division, without separation; the distinction . . . being in no way abolished because of the union, but rather the characteristic property of each . . . being preserved.' In fact, we can go even further than Chalcedon. With a community – whether it's the Trinity or the Church – the 'characteristic property' of each individual isn't just preserved: it's *enhanced*.

This is the thrust of Pat Lynch's book. Tracing the idea of community from its roots in the Trinity, through the Bible and Church history, Pat is clear: 'No Christian is a Christian in complete isolation'. It's a timely and essential message that Christians of all persuasions need to hear. Because when the Church – in all its various genuine forms – takes it fully on board, we'll have so much more to give to the rest of the world. The fragmentation of modern society is clearly visible, and its results are potentially catastrophic. 'There is the desire for community,' Pat states, 'but the experience of aliena-tion.' By drawing on our strength as one body, Christians can 'offer Christ, and a realistic, healthy, practical and lived prophetic com-munity' to a world that so desperately needs it. There could be no message more relevant to the hour than this. I commend it to you.

Rev. Steve Chalke
International Director, Oasis Trust

Introduction

This book has come into existence because of a desire on my part to look critically and positively at the whole area of community once again. As I write it I am aware that the fabric of stability in the Church and in many countries is falling apart. Frequently people I meet stop and ask why this is so. This book is but an attempt, among others, at an answer; the loss of community and the progress into even deeper individualism. There is a growing isolation in the Church and in the world which is fragmenting the faith community and pulling society apart. The pace of life and the sudden changes that have occurred, particularly in the area of technology, serve only to cement isolation. The collapse in the family unit has left people exhausted and unsupported. Crime is on the increase on our streets and there is sin and corruption in leadership in the religious and secular worlds. Even the families that hang together shoulder a kind of quiet desperation.

But I do not want to be a prophet of doom. This book is about community and how it has been the intention of the Creator from the beginning. In God we have the model; in ourselves we have the desire for selfishness. The pull between the two gives us the 'unresolved tension' of my title. The structure and limitations of this book will be seen at a glance from the Contents page. This book is not meant to give a full-scale praxis of community. I have limited myself to looking again at the origins of community, its development down through the ages and its universal call to all of us. This book is certainly not meant to give a blueprint for action, but merely a call to leave our individualism and move towards community, whatever this may mean for each of us. It seems to me that the answers to many of today's problems lie in models of community. However, as to the correctness of this statement and indeed this book, I leave that for the reader to judge. I am well aware that there are huge gaps in this book but this must not deter us in our examination of the problems and in our attempt at a solution – community.

The situation in the Church is not all bleak. There are many good and constructive things happening. There are many new communities sprouting up all over the world. These vary in construction and in structure. The communities that are already in existence are trying desperately hard to revamp themselves so that they can become more relevant to a changing society. As I travel worldwide I see the pain and fruits of such communities. What I do see is that there is no decline in interest in community. In the communities that have collapsed there has been great pain and hurt because people have put their lives on the line. Many others succeed because they have paid close attention to their quality of leadership, their ability to take direction and the nature and depth of their commitment. The risks are so great but the fruits are so productive.

I value living in a Christian community. The family unit and environment in which I was brought up in Buncrana,

INTRODUCTION

County Donegal, Ireland, was a real community. I owe an immense gratitude to my family and the neighbours of my youth. The Catholic Church also showed me that Christian community is vital to healthy living and ministry. If I am at all critical of her it is only because I love her so much. From the Catholic Church I learnt the meaning of community and the place of my priesthood within it. As a result I had little trouble moving into Sion Catholic Community who have continued the teaching process.

This community for evangelisation has reinforced the necessity of community living with all its pain. I have found that living within it has helped to channel my lifestyle and my ministry away from individualism and towards the corporate. Much of my life involves teaching and preaching and therefore living out of a suitcase, so it is very important for me to be 'sent' by my community and to return home again to a family atmosphere. Community also alleviates the isolation and loneliness which is so much a part of today's culture.

1

A Community of Three

Some time ago I received a letter from a young married couple in their mid-thirties.

> Life has been very good to us. We have a very good background and are not without a penny or two. We have two children and are involved in the modern rat race that some people call the 'yuppie society'.
>
> We had a conversion experience in our local church – would you believe through the ministry of a Catholic priest? Since then things have gone well but over the last few months God seems to be getting at us again. We are not content with the 'fellowshipping' that we are experiencing. It does not go deep enough for us. We are feeling that there is something more. We are aware that what we are seeking may be community but this word is not used very much in our church. We are aware also that community is made up of individuals, but also transcends them by incorporating them into a more exclusive whole. Could you help us understand where this deep calling is coming from?

This young couple's search is for an enhanced identity and

a sense of belonging, without ceasing to be individuals. This is not unusual today. However, one could ask, 'What gives the Christian community identity?' If community is not to be an aggregate of individuals, it must have some principles that hold it together.[1] Any community, like the individual, derives its sense of identity from a remembered past and an anticipated future. It is this sense of remembered past that is of interest to us here.

Throughout history, questions have focused on 'Who we are and where we are going'. The human situation places heavy burdens of fashioning meaning for our lives out of the raw material of personal and collective experience. Where the human situation is concerned, it is clear why the problem of God is perennial. However we conceive God, our vision will always be that of a 'perfect' being.[2] God is a concept expressing what it would be like to have the creative and the transcendent in our human grasp. God represents a resolution to the contradiction we humans feel within ourselves. We are split and disunited beings. God is whole and perfect. At minimum God is the answer to the human dilemma.

Our quest for meaning is seeking to find a satisfying answer to the question, 'From where do we come?' We are historical beings. The meaning we find in human and social community cannot be separated from a knowledge that our present is grounded in a significant past. People are searching for their roots. There is an increasing fad of genealogical research. I find it interesting that it is within the societies most automised, most pluralised, most materialised, most secularised that the genealogist is kept most busy. This speaks of a society no longer able to inspire a deep sense of purpose and hence individuals will seek that sense grounded in personal family history. The historian works to create a story which enables a community or nation to understand its roots.

On another level, the evolutionary scientist seeks to unlock the mystery of the origin of species, the earth and the universe itself. There is a great interest in this type of research.[3] The fact that gifted men and women devote their lives to this is evidence of the importance we place on the question, 'From where?' But we want more than this. Understanding the process of evolution can only go so far in satisfying our personal quest. In essence we are asking a different question from that which science can provide. It is in answering this question that the meaning of God can be found. It is in ascribing 'Creator' to God that we will find meaning and purpose in the universe, our world, our community and in our individual lives. God reflects the deepest longing of the human person.

God as Creator

The idea of God as Father appears to be increasingly unpopular. Yet we call God 'Father' and speak of him as the source of all that is. The very mention of the word 'father' can send out all sorts of signals today. The father – especially in Hebrew society – is the one with authority, the one who is in control of the family. The father is also the judge who must arbitrate family disputes; the good father is neither tyrannical nor of a legal nature. A family is bound together into a special form of community in which the role of the father should be one of love; his justice not the exercise of harsh and inflexible law but rather tempered with mercy and forgiveness. To call God 'Father' is, therefore, to imply that his 'fatherhood' is exercised for the welfare of his children, while retaining ultimate power, ultimate authority, ultimate rights (Luke 15:11–32).

As the Father Creator, God is dependent on nothing outside himself for his creativity; neither in materials or training, nor inspiration of some muse or blind chance. In his freedom he produces what he wills. It is this incomprehensible majesty and mystery of God's fatherhood over the world that we read in the opening words of Genesis:

In the beginning God created the heavens and the earth. Now the earth was a formless void, there was darkness over the deep, and God's spirit hovered over the waters. God said, 'Let there be light', and there was light. (Gen. 1:1–3)

Yet it has also to be said that God loves the Son so much that everything is created in the image and likeness of Jesus.

Blessed be God the Father of our Lord Jesus Christ, who has blessed us with all the spiritual blessings of heaven in Christ. Before the world was made, he chose us, chose us in Christ, to be holy and spotless, and to live through love in his presence, determining that we should become his adopted sons, through Jesus Christ for his own kind purposes, to make us praise the glory of his grace, his free gift to us in the Beloved, in whom, through his blood, we gain our freedom, the forgiveness of our sins. (Eph. 1:3–7)

Logically, therefore, creation took place in and through community. If I create something – say, a painting – it comes to have a certain independence from me. Without me it could not have come into existence but it can still exist if I sell it or give it away. It no longer needs me to exist. If the painting changes in time, as it shall, this will not be due to my creativity but to the creativeness or destruction of others. Hence if everything is created by God and created for community we are at liberty to enhance or destroy it.

If God is the Creator then he is the foundation on which everything is grounded. This means that we cannot possibly escape from him without ceasing to be. However, our un-faith is the root of our anxieties, fears and despairs. If we have real faith in the Creator then we gain an understanding of community which is synonymous with our Creator who operates out of the Trinity.

The Trinity: The Constituents of Community

The Father, the Son, and the Holy Spirit are extolled and worshipped together in one breath. The Apostles' Creed calls God 'Father' twice: first at creation, 'I believe in God the Father . . . maker of heaven and earth'; second after Christ's ascension, 'He sits at the right hand of the Father.'

a) *God the Father of Jesus*

God the Father is defined here by his relationship to the Son. Therefore, in the Christian understanding of God as Father, what is meant is simply and exclusively 'the Father of the Son Jesus Christ'. It is the Father of Jesus whom we believe and acknowledge as the Creator of the world. It is in this Trinitarian sense that God is understood as Father. It is possible, therefore, that it is only when we are in relationship with the only begotten Son that we will be able to recognise what the divine fatherhood really means. The name 'Father' here is a theological term and not a biological one. If God is the Father of Jesus and if he is only 'our Father' for Jesus's sake, then we can only call him 'Abba' in the spirit of free sons and daughters.

> Everyone moved by the Spirit is a son of God. The spirit you received is not the spirit of slaves bringing fear into your lives again; it is the spirit of sons and it makes us cry out 'Abba, Father!' The Spirit himself and our spirit bear united witness that we are children of God. And if we are children we are heirs as well: heirs of God and coheirs with Christ, sharing his sufferings so as to share his glory. (Rom. 8:14–17)

The ambiguity that can exist between the Father of Jesus Christ and the Father of the universe needs to be clarified, which is why I have written about the Father as Creator. When the Creator is called 'Father' what is meant in Christian terms is that creation proceeds from the Father through the Son. This means that the creation is manifestly an act of Trinity and therefore one of community. According to the Council of Toledo in 675, it is held that the Son was created neither out of nothingness nor yet out of any substance but that he was begotten of the Father's very essence.[4] In this eternal begetting and birth of the Son, God proves himself to be a Father. The Son and the Spirit proceed from the Father but the Father proceeds from no other divine person. We can say that he is without origin or beginning. We see then that the origin of the Trinity is the Father.[5] However, when we talk about order of origin in the Trinity we have to underline its uniqueness when compared with anything else. It is keeping these differences in mind that I am here using this concept of origin.

b) *Who Is the Son?*

The Son is the 'only begotten' eternal Son of the Father.[6] He is not created 'out of nothing' but proceeds from the substance of the Father. Therefore, the Son is one in substance and essence with the Father and has everything in common with him, except the Father's 'personal' characteristics. The world is the creation of the Father (Gen. 1). Human beings are made in God's image.[7] The world and all it contains is God's greatest desire and not the subject of self-realisation. It is in communion with the first-born of all creation that the world is called into the community life of God (Eph. 1:3–7). It is only in relationship with Jesus that men and women are drawn into God's life and into community.

The Father who generates and brings forth communicates everything to Jesus his Son – that is, everything except his fatherhood. What is communicated then is his divinity, his power and his glory. His fatherhood cannot be communicated; otherwise the Son would be a second Father. The Son receives his divinity and his being as a Person from the Father. He is not the origin of the Godhead. This cannot be so because if it were there would be two such origins in the Trinity. The 'birth' of the Son comes from the very nature of God the Father, not from his will. The Son then, like the Father, belongs to the eternal constitution of the Trinity. This eternal 'birth' springs from the Father's necessity of being.[8] The love that is shared between Father and Son is dynamic.

The Father loves the Son with a Fatherly love while the Son loves the Father with a responsive, self-giving love. This love which the Father has for the Son is open for creation and is in harmony with his fatherhood. It is creative love. It calls things into life – beings made in the image of the Son who are in communion with the Son and therefore return the Father's love. Creation was destined to be in harmony and obedience to love and so give glory to the Trinity.

Because Jesus is the only-begotten Son, he is the bearer of divine revelation: 'Jesus said: I am the Way; the Truth and the Life. No one can come to the Father except through me' (John 14:6). As the revealer of God, Jesus is 'the Son' and he belongs so closely to our knowledge of God as God that we can no longer think of God apart from Jesus. By sending Jesus, God shows that he is a God of love and also that love is his nature. The Son's response to eternal love is his obedience on Calvary. The fact that the Son died on a cross is a sign of the self-giving love that is called for in any community.

c) *Who Is the Holy Spirit?*
In dealing with the terms 'Father' and 'Son' an immediate understanding of terminology can be gleaned. Both of these words are relationship-orientated. However, when I use the words 'Holy Spirit' of the third Person of the Trinity then a certain difference can be experienced. We read in the Gospel of John that 'God is Spirit' (John 4:24). Therefore, spirit is a description of divine existence. The word 'Holy' does not adequately describe the third Person of the Trinity because God is holy. Theologians like Thomas Aquinas thought the third Person of the Trinity had no name of his own but that which was given to him by biblical usage.[9] Maybe that is why in Christian art the Father and the Son are represented by two persons and the Holy Spirit as a dove.

The concept of the Holy Spirit is difficult in terms of his

origin. The Spirit is 'breathed forth' and therefore not begotten. The Spirit cannot be a second Son. If this were so the Son would be a second Father and there would be two different origins for the Holy Spirit. We know that the Father utters his eternal Word:

> In the beginning was the Word: the Word was with God and the Word was God. He was with God in the beginning. Through him all things came to be, not one thing had its being but through him. (John 1:1–3)

This is the breathing out of his Spirit. There is in God no Word without the Spirit and no Spirit without the Word. With this in mind, the Spirit and Jesus are indissolubly linked. It is traditionally held that the Holy Spirit together with the Word (Son) proceeds from the Father. The Father is then the origin of the Godhead. If this is so then the Holy Spirit is not created but he issues forth from the Father. The Holy Spirit is then of the same essence and substance as the Father and the Son. When we experience the Holy Spirit we experience God himself.

John 15:26 tells us that the Spirit of truth proceeds from the Father but is 'sent' by Jesus. According to John 14:26, the Father 'sent' the Spirit in Christ's name. If this is so then the Holy Spirit proceeds from the Father and the Son and is uniquely linked to both in communion. The Nicene Creed affirms that the Spirit is of one nature with the Father and the Son, and with the Father and Son equally worshipped and glorified. The three Persons of the Trinity – Father, Son and Spirit – are indissolubly linked together in the unity of divine love.

The Trinity : A Dynamic Community

The idea of unity is primarily an arithmetical one: the criterion of unity is the absence of multiplicity. In our thinking one is one and three are three. What is one is not three and what is three is not one.[10] We have long been acquainted with unities which are not so simple. There is, for example, aesthetic unity – the unity of a work of art. There is organic unity – the unity of a living creature. In both of these, the unity is far from being simple. It does indeed include certain kinds of multiplicity, such as a distracting multiplicity of interests in a work of art, or a lack of co-ordination in the activities of a living creature. But it can only exist at all by virtue of the presence of another kind of multiplicity; the multiplicity of the varied elements which constitute the work of art or the living creature. Each organism is an arithmetical unity in respect of being a single member of the world of organisms in general. But it only exists as unifying in a single life history the various elements of which it is composed; elements which can only play their part in that life if they are different from and complementary to one another.

If the degree of unity is thus to be measured by a scale of intensity of unifying power, it is not by decreasing the number or the variety of the elements by which the unity will be heightened but rather the reverse. The person who can only achieve selfhood by concentrating on a narrow selection of interests is one who is weak in unifying power. Life is far more intense when a wide range is unified. According to the revelation of himself which God has given us in history, there are three elements perfectly united in the divine life and each of these elements is itself a Person.

It is the main thesis of this book that the act of community requires an acceptance of the doctrine of the Trinity; that the divine unity is a dynamic unity actively unifying in the one divine life the lives of three divine Persons. This is a mystery, but not an irrational mystery. It is a mystery because at this moment on earth we have little experience of this type of unity which so perfectly draws together so wide and rich a diversity of content. Our experience does not go beyond the imperfect unification of activities in our single personal selves and we by no means fully understand that.

> In many modern societies it is deemed necessary to test the abilities and aptitudes of individuals. But what any one of us can do is directly related to our social environment and in particular whether we are living in a climate of appreciation or discouragement or indifference.[11]

The Godhead is the perfect example of the kind of unity of which we have imperfect analogies on earth; for example, marriage, covenanted communities and others. How mysterious, tremendous and fascinating – we argue – must be the intensity of the unifying power which constitutes the unity of the blessed Trinity. The Christian doctrine of God then contains an assertion about the nature of community. It asserts that all the actual unities of our earthly experience – from the unity of science to the unity of a work of art, of the human self, or of a human society – are imperfect instances of what community truly is. We may find in them analogies to that true unity and learn from them something of what perfect unity must be. Perfect unity is to be found only in God and casts light on our lesser unities. Thus the revelation of the Trinity with its contribution to human thought on the subject of community should be appreciated as an historical fact and a source of enlightenment.

Qualities of a Communing God

I gave a retreat recently to a particular community. On the surface, things seemed to be running smoothly; but when I shared at a deep level with individuals I realised that great tensions existed at the core of their corporate life. The community was struggling with loyalty, friendship and understanding. These areas of difficulty being experienced are the basic qualities needed to build a healthy and vibrant community.

a) *Faithfulness*

The first perfection of divine communing is God's faithfulness. Faithfulness, like most terms used of God in this chapter, is drawn from interpersonal relationships. It denotes the steadfastness in loyalty characteristic of a true friend. A faithful friend is one who keeps faith regardless of impulses or pressure to the contrary. A faithful friend binds themself to you in such a way that you can rely on them. You can be certain that they will not desert or betray you in that desperate hour when you need them. A faithful friend is one who deliberately sustains community with another even at severe cost to themself.

'Abba (Father) . . . everything is possible for you. Take this cup away from me. But let it be as you, not I, would have it' (Mark 14:36–7). The friend has sufficient force of will to sustain the community from their side regardless of the threat. Of course we do not know faithfulness in this ideal sense. We are finite beings and unavoidably let others down. Some of the most poignant 'betrayals' by loved ones are unwilled. In this context something of the faithfulness of God can be understood. God has revealed himself to be both powerful enough and loving always to be faithful. God's faithfulness comes from the unity in community. His power and his love are not abstracts but concrete reality in actual human lives. God's faithfulness, of course, is not restricted to his dealings with people; his keeping faith with human-kind is a symbol of his relations within the Trinity.[12] God's faithfulness is the presence of his spirit to and with all creation; sustaining it in being, giving it structure. God's faithfulness is such that all creation, especially we humans, can move towards the realisation of ultimate objectives – community. The stability and dependability which we find in God is an expression of Trinitarian community.

b) *Responsiveness*

The second perfection of divine communing is respon-siveness. Again this term is drawn from interpersonal relationships. Some would consider responsiveness as part of faithfulness. How could we be faithful to one who is not responsive? However, among one's friends one can distin-guish some who are more responsive than others. This is no reflection on their faithfulness. Rather it points to sensitivity in their attitude to the needs of others. The responsive friend has the delicate art of knowing when the right moment is around. Faithfulness alone may not be enough, for it is responsiveness that gives relationships spontaneity, life and vitality. However, a relationship that is characterised by responsiveness alone could be no more than a mechanical reaction. Both faithfulness and responsiveness are necessary to ensure community. The 'I' and 'You' need to be in communion. We can speak then of God's responsiveness as well as his faithfulness. God's ways are to respond.

> The man Jesus is not only the one sent by the Holy Trinity, He is also the representation and highest fulfilment of the human response of love to God's courtship.[13]

God's responsiveness in the community of the Trinity enables him to deal with every new happening in the created order with freshness and creativity. God's responsiveness and faithfulness are experienced in community through loyalty.

c) *Understanding*

The third perfection of divine communing is understanding. A frequent cry today in our society is about the lack of understanding. God's response can be faithful because he knows us perfectly. God has omniscience and empathy for others. We say that God deals with his creation in understanding because he treats his creatures wisely, not ignorantly or rigidly nor without due consideration of our characters and our natures. His action towards us is characterised by sympathy.

> It was essential that he should in this way become completely like his brothers so that he could be a compassionate ... high priest ... able to help others who are tempted. (Heb. 2:17–18)

When our sympathetic understanding of others helps make possible their free emergence as created persons in

17

responsible community, it becomes an analogue for grasping the significance of God's understanding of himself in the community of the Trinity and of all his creation.

Our Response

The experience of estrangement is foreign to community and, therefore, foreign to God as Trinity. Humans were created for community with God and with each other. The God of love forgives us and restores us back into community. The forgiveness of God is an expression of the intimacy of his Spirit to us. Forgiveness is wiping away the distance that has come between us in community. In my community I have found that when there is a lack of forgiveness then trust and confidence are violated, to mention but a few of its effects.

Forgiveness is the response of God and it should be the first response in any community. Yet this is so hard to do because we have to swallow our pride. Forgiveness resumes communion. Because it is such a delicate act, full and free forgiveness seldom occurs among us humans. Our forgiveness is usually tentative and fearful and half-hearted. The Trinity, however, has perfect understanding, perfect love and abounding freedom. God, therefore, can deal with humans in perfect forgiveness, reconstituting the situation that we have corrupted and making it possible for us to live community.

> Jesus' personal 'ABBA' relationship expresses his sending by the Father in time, a commission which He accepted in obedience.
>
> And this manifests the eternal relation of the Son to the Father and hence indirectly the eternal . . . Deity of the Son . . . and the Trinitarian mystery of the whole.[14]

The Trinity : A Relevant Community

We live in a genuinely secular world. Our forebears had a sense of God's continuous providential guidance throughout history. They found their lives to be meaningful because each person had their unique place and task. 'Late Western civilisation, it is said, is the only major civilisation known to us in which atheism became an acceptable, and hence a widespread cultural option.'[15]

For some people our present-day loss of a transcendent source and purpose has made human life meaningless or even absurd – a pointless and empty burden simply to be endured. Some have reacted with bitterness and revulsion.

> To have lost God means madness, and when mankind will discover that it has lost God, universal madness will break out. This apocalyptic sense of dreadful things to come hangs over Nietzsche's thinking like a thundercloud.[16]

Others seem to find sufficient satisfaction in the daily round of activities punctuated occasionally by experience of unusual excitement not to miss or lament the dimensions of depth and mystery in which previous generations found their lives ensconced.

> Russell's thought . . . moved towards the 'reasonable belief' experiment and what one might call faith in the realm of ethics and social philosophy but not in religion.[17]

It is little wonder that our age finds it dubious to undertake a general search for God. How can the Trinity have specific meaning in a secular world where community is desired but selfishness is prevalent?

For the Christian, however, God as community is the source and ground of all that is. From this perspective everything in the created universe, every experience can be understood in relation to the Trinity. If we as Christians fail to see this fact then our roots will always be erroneous. 'For everything comes from God alone. Everything lives by his power and everything is for his glory' (Rom. 11:36 *Living Bible*).

It is necessary then to see the character of the world, with all its richness of complexities, as expressing the unfolding Trinity. This is required if the Christian faith truly has as its object the God of all that is, and not mere wordy abstractions which bear little or no relation to the concrete reality of life. God is working out his purposes in and through the world in which we find ourselves. The world's very existence is an expression of his purposeful activity in creation. Thus both the existence and the character of all finite events and beings are to be understood finally by reference to God's purposes.

The Trinitarian relationship between God and the world can be understood in the concept of *purpose*. The word 'purpose' can be understood as the power to connect together successive moments into an organic unity by carrying through a plan of development. This notion of purpose expresses the relationship that God has with his world. We affirm that precisely this world in which we live has its being only because of God's activity. It is only when we see it in this way that we are able to interpret that we exist out of community in creation and that we are moving towards community at death. This reality of 'last things' sets forth the end goal of being with God, to which all of creation is moving.

'For modern secular man death is the end . . . It forces him to ask "Has the individual a glorious destiny?" '[18] When we grasp this pertinent fact we can see very clearly that the main object of human endeavour is to build community. This can be done religiously, scientifically, materially, politically, socially or medically, to mention but a few ways. The rationale then for us Christians must be the mystery of the Trinity of inclusion. Leonardo Boff expresses it very well when he writes:

> If God were one alone, there would be solitude and concentration in unity and oneness. If God were two, a duality, Father and Son only, there would be a separation (one being distinct from the other), and exclusion (one not being the other). But God is *three*, a Trinity, and being three avoids solitude, overcomes separation and surpasses exclusion. The Trinity allows identity (the Father) difference of identity (the Son) and difference of difference (the Holy Spirit). Trinity prevents face to face confrontation between Father and Son in a 'narcissistic' contemplation. The third figure (Holy Spirit) is the difference, the openness, communion . . . single and multiple, unity and diversity meet in the Trinity.[19]

Because of this unity of communion in the Trinity, we need to know what type of society is in line with God's plan. The question can be asked, 'Is the form of social organisation we have at this time really pleasing to God?' We could say that our ability to share leaves a lot to be desired; our society is becoming more and more individualistic with an increasing growth of materialism. There are cries for justice from all areas of society. The inspiration for all of this derives its meaning from the Trinity which is the embodiment of an ideal society. The Trinity can be seen as a model for any just, equal and self-respecting organisation.

On the basis of our faith, we Christians are called to live out the likeness of the Trinity. This will entail participation, equality and community that will be a prophetic lamp to the isolationist, the poor, the oppressed and many others on the lowest levels of society and the Church. No disunited society can create favourable conditions to express the mystery of the Trinity. Through the transcendence of God we humans are called to be rooted in something greater than ourselves – the Trinity. The Trinity and its transcendence form the unity of our existence.

> Finally the whole Trinity contains creation in itself. Communion is the first and last word about the mystery of the Trinity. Translating this truth of faith into social terms, we can say 'the Trinity is our true social programme'.[20]

2

The Community of Original Blessings

Sion Community, the community to which I belong, spends at least six weeks on in-service training each year. One topic that we try to address is how to make community life more holistic, meaningful and productive. During these sessions we speculate as to what it must have been like before the Fall, when things moved in harmony – perfect community. 'God saw all he had made, and indeed it was very good' (Gen. 1:31).

A Universe in Harmony

The physical observable creation is, at root, all good. Human beings are, equally rootedly, all good. There was at the initial creation no outer part of the universe and no inner part of the self which possessed a moral status which was at variance with the status of any other part. There was no hidden element either far out in some uncharted area of space or hidden deep within the recesses of the human which was dark and out of control. There was no element of God's creation which derived life from an alien source other than the Maker's goodness.

'Christians and people of many other religions believe that there is a God who created the Universe and everything in it.'[1] The entire universe, together with the entirety of the human race within the universe was at one with itself and was rooted in the divine.[2] The realisation that this is the case is the beginning of wisdom and destiny. It is the beginning of wisdom about God and also the beginning of wisdom about people and our original self-worth. It is the wisdom which, when taken radically, releases health of body, soul and mind. It releases peace and justice between peoples and the created order and sows the seeds for building community.

In the Genesis narratives, creation is the activity of God. We are recalled to our proper understanding of community and to its true and original condition. Creation is the establishment of relatedness, of dependence and inter-dependence. It is a work of love rather than power. On successive days the different parts of the creation are set in relationship one to another. But at the core of it all is God: 'God said, "Let there be . . ." ' (Gen. 1). God then is the source of relationships. Creation reveals an act of order and a process of giving things and people their true nature.

Again and again it [creation] is the undistorted place where man is, remote from all imaginations and dreams and especially from all religious phantoms, so that the listener can understand, in terms of the world as it is, God's nature, his actions and the significance of his reign.[3]

A creation-based understanding of community is necessary to those who would escape the dislocations of modern

Western consciousness. Thomas Merton puts it like this:

> The doctrine of creation is ... that which implies the deepest respect for reality and for the being of everything that is ... [it] is rooted not in a desperate religious attempt to account for the fact that the world exists. It is not merely an answer to the question of how things got to be what they are ... On the contrary the doctrine of creation starts not from a question about being but from a direct institution of the act of being ...[4]

From the above we can see that a preoccupation with 'being' alone will lead us into selfishness, but a realisation about the 'act of being' will root us in God and altruism. This universe and all its inhabitants are grounded in God. 'All that exists comes from him; all is by him and for him' (Rom. 11:36).

The original character of this universe can be deduced directly from the nature of God, namely harmonious and united. It is a fundamental ethical principle, therefore, that reverence for all things needs to be observed. The inanimate as well as the organic world is God's creation and has its place within his purposes. In the original order of things it was honoured and respected. It was not exploited, defaced or destroyed. There was an awe and respect for all creation, giving each creature its due and reviling none. 'The way we combine these aspects of God's creative activity has important consequences for the value we set on creation and so for our practical attitudes.'[5]

Creator and Creatures in Harmony

The term 'creation' does not include only the action of the Creator but also its product, the creature. Creator and creature belong together as an integral whole. The Genesis story makes it quite clear that man and woman are placed by God in the world which God has created. It is clear that the creation of man and woman (Gen. 1:26–31) is presented differently from the preceding works of creation. The passage is set apart from what has taken place before by a new introduction: 'Let us make man . . .' (Gen 1:26). What is common to the structure of the other works of creation is missing here. The creation of man and woman does not appear as creation through the Word. The word 'us' is used of God. We can deduce from this that man and woman are meant for community because their origin is specifically community.

These verses of Genesis sum up what it means to be human: we are what we are precisely as a creature of God; Adam and Eve's creature state determined their compatibility and the meaning of their existence. What they were capable of was bestowed upon them as a blessing. What God had decided to create must stand in relationship to him. The creation of man and woman in God's image is directed to something happening between God and humans. The Creator created creatures that correspond to him, to whom he can speak, and who can learn from him. It must be noted here that creation is plural.

Creation of humans in the image of God is not concerned with the individual but with the species. This means, surely, that humans are created for community with each other and communion with God. It is amazing that a single phrase, 'God created man in the image of himself,' can be so misunderstood. If we do not understand that the declaration here about humans is plural and community-orientated, then we can quickly develop a theology of individualism. The biblical declaration about the dignity of man and woman differs from the secular view in that it says something not only about human worth but also about the meaning of human existence; everyone is created for this purpose, namely that something may happen between humans and God and thereby life may receive a meaning.

A Family in Harmony

Perhaps it would be more logical to look closely at who Adam and Eve were as human beings before we look at what they were intended to become. But this is not the way God's logic works. In God's arithmetic things begin from the other end. They begin with God's action in a holistic and perfect creation of humanity.[6] God is a Utopian God, because humans were God's Utopia. This Utopia was a life of participation, communion, community, partnership and mutual understanding.

The Bible narratives of Genesis 1 and 2 look at man and woman in all their essential relationships. Man and woman are not merely human because they were made. Many other things are required, not least the community dimension. There is also their relationship to God and its consequences for human existence. In the creation story man is created before woman. He was provided with every kind of nourishment and received a commission and thereby an occupation which should have given meaning to his life. 'Yahweh God took the man and settled him in the garden of Eden to cultivate and take care of it' (Gen. 2:15–16). But was this living? Was this really the idea of humanity that God intended? The question is answered by God himself, 'It is not good that the man should be alone' (Gen. 2:18).

Could it be that God wants to set solitary existence against community? 'It is not good that man should be alone' expresses clearly that the characteristic of being human is not found in mere existence as a solitary man. It can only be found in community. The first man has all the provisions he needs. He is being taken care of. But is this good? God answers the question in the negative and we are presented with the necessity of community for proper human development. To fulfil the desire for community God brings all living creatures to the man but none of them satisfies Adam (Gen. 2:18–21). He demonstrates his autonomy by discovering, defining and ordering the world. But for him 'no helpmate suitable . . . was found' (Gen. 2:21). So God creates a woman.

'But the fundamental thing is that women are more like men than anything else in the world. They are human beings.'[7] With the coming together of Adam and Eve we have in essence the beginnings of human community. This is our first description of human community and is so vital to the present day.

> Better two than one by himself, since thus their work is really profitable. If one should fall, the other helps him up; but woe to the man by himself with no one to help him up when he falls down. Again: they keep warm who sleep two together, but how can man keep warm alone? Where one alone would be overcome, two will put up resistance; and a threefold cord is not quickly broken. (Eccles. 4:9–12)

Adam greets Eve with a cry. This exclamation is an expression of his joyful surprise in the companionship of woman. 'This at last is bone from my bones and flesh from my flesh! This is to be called woman' (Gen. 2:23). He is living in community. There is the basic love of man for woman and woman for man. We see the strongest bond which causes two human beings to seek and belong to each other. One could ask, what is being said here about the relationship of man and woman? What is the basic form of human relationships? The answer must take into account the whole area of human existence. It is not just about the mutual love with its basic power of bringing two people into close union in a new community. It is about a community of life where each is so suited to the other that they mutually correspond with each other in naturalness of being. The Bible tells us little about the experience of Adam and Eve within this state of perfection. However, I am going to speculate on the reality of life for this first community.

One with the Creator

Adam and Eve, although free, were inseparable from the living, personal God. An obvious implication of this fact is that in reality they were completely dependent upon God for their existence. However, Adam and Eve were not only creatures but persons which implies relative independence and the ability to make decisions and set goals. This meant that they possessed a great degree of freedom – at least in the sense of being able to make choices. God did not create robots whose courses were totally determined by forces outside of themselves. They had the power of self-determination and self-direction. They were people of options.

From Genesis 1:27 we may infer that another aspect of

their unity with God is in the fact that God created them male and female. I do not conclude, however, that their resemblance with God is founded in the physical difference between men and women, but rather in the fact that Adam needed community and is therefore a social being. In this way, human beings reflect God who exists not as a solitary being but rather as community. In this way Adam and Eve reflected God in that they were persons, responsible beings, who could be addressed by God and who were ultimately responsible to God as their Creator. God in the Scriptures is revealed as a Person who is able to make decisions and to rule, so Adam and Eve are persons who are likewise able to make decisions and to rule.

Man and woman came from the hands of the Creator and were not corrupt, depraved or sinful. They were in a state of integrity, innocence and holiness. They were created to relate first to their Maker and then to each other. Humans in isolation from God were never envisaged. Our continued and corporate existence is lost when we do not continue to breathe God's breath and when we do not touch the living life of God. Whatever in human beings today is evil or perverted was not part of the original creation. In our original blessings we were 'very good'.

One with Each Other

In the context of Genesis 2 it is clear that Adam is very enthusiastic about God's work, especially the creation of a 'helpmate'. The creation of woman from the rib of man is not intended in any derogatory sense. The word 'rib' indicates that man and woman are the same in nature. Among Arabs today, a man will speak of someone really close to him as his 'rib'.

The establishment of the first family indicates the need of human beings for social life and the means of fulfilling the commission from God to multiply. In creating woman and linking her closely to man, God created one flesh which was the source of perfect community. The making of community is much deeper than any modern idea of companionship. Contemporary thinkers could discuss the social organisation of this first community with hostility because this structure apparently oppresses women.

This structure did not sustain unhealthy subordination but rather is one of total perfect union. This first community was one of intimacy, which implies warmth, kindness and love, which humankind has sought ever since the Fall. Because of the nature of this first community, impassioned searching, aloneness, failure and despair did not exist. Communication and the abilities to accept difference and to share in intimacy would have been among the attributes of this unique union. This first human community was, therefore, based upon constructive relationships born of primal innocence. Both partners must have lived an idyllic relationship. Sex would not have been used selfishly or as a means of domination, but rather to liberate and free. Harmony would have prevailed.

This first community of Adam and Eve was a union of values, the by-products of which were self-investment in relationships and the willingness to give freely as well as to take. 'Style of life ... suggests that ... faith is lived not only in the realm of work, not only in the so-called orders of creation or in the public realm, but in privacy as well.'[8] I contend that this first couple had a true enlightenment which transcended their egocentric interest. They were involved in a genuine caring for each other. The battle for equal rights for women and men is a central issue of our contemporary scene. In this first union of Adam and Eve the uniqueness of their biological make-up did not presuppose inequality. Adam and Eve were not the same but yet equal. This meant that their equality of personhood, like that of the Triune God, gave them a right to their own individuality, to their difference that made them unique. This equality of responsibility for self meant that both of them had an equal right to free each other so that their personal needs and desires resulted in fulfilment and growth. They would have naturally granted each other such equality as man and woman and were therefore peers.

They would have had no fears about their relative status in their union because their starting point would have been that of equality. Their union would not have been restricted by the false demands of a closed mentality. Because of this equality, the forcing of an unnatural sameness upon each other never occurred but rather their uniqueness was paramount. Their individuality would have given them stature, not status. Because they gave each other this stature there were almost no boundaries to what they could do together. They were open and equal to be part of the creativeness of God.[9]

One with Nature
Because their relationship was healthy they had the energy and motivation for involvement in their world. Their creative intimacy would have been a propellant to get constructively involved in their natural surroundings. The first creation story of Genesis (1:1–31) has an important message for us. The story is a powerful proclamation that there is a fundamental relationship between God and the whole of created

matter. The whole of creation is to be understood in terms of relationships. Humans are given dominion over the animals and told to subdue the earth. God said: 'Be masters of the fish of the sea, the birds of heaven and all living animals on the earth . . . I give all the foliage of plants for food' (Gen. 1:28–32).

For our ears today, this is harsh language. However, in its original context it would have had a liberating intention. Here, unlike other ancient creation narratives where humans are seen as slaves of their God, humans are given a dominant role. The language of domination must always be interpreted in the light of understanding that humanity is made in the image of God the Creator, as we have seen above. This Creator takes delight in all creatures. So this dominion has no justification for ruthless exploitation and irresponsible destruction of the created earth. Such behaviour is immoral and certainly not at one with creation or the Creator.

The command given to the newly made human beings in Genesis 2:15 is to 'cultivate and take care of' the Garden of Eden. The first duty of humanity was to dress the garden, till it, manage it, keep and protect it. This could be described as '*oikas*', ecology. 'The Greeks used the word OIKAS to describe a home, a place to which you could return and where you understood and were familiar with the local environment.'[10] The ultimate ownership of the world was never doubted by Adam and Eve. They had a subordinate role to God, and there is no suggestion of ownership at the time of creation – rather of man and woman in partnership with the created order. There is no suggestion that humans would inherit the earth for themselves as a reward for good management. They were at one with nature. 'And hereby man was invested with the power . . . to preserve the face of the Earth, in beauty, usefulness and fruitfulness.'[11]

The Origin of Discord

A command is given to Adam in the garden. He could eat of
any tree in the garden except one. All other statements by
the Creator seem perfectly reasonable and intelligible to
Adam except this one. All that he should do was to listen
and obey. Yet even though this command was given to Adam
it was broken by both himself and Eve. This introduces a
new concept: man is now in a position to accept or reject
God's commands. In the creation story the command to obey
offers man the possibility of loyalty. The sin of disobedience
which broke that Utopian bond between God and humankind was committed by both Adam and Eve. As community
they broke with the perfect community of the Trinity.

We see that community can be seduced amid all the
goodness that God has created. In the temptation the way
seems to be open to humans to be like God. 'You will be
like gods' says the serpent (Gen. 3:5). It is true defection.
The woman moves outside of her community with God and
she assents. Adam broke with God by complicity. Human
beings are shown here as ready to avoid responsibility and
allow themselves to drift. The man's leadership qualities
which are necessary for the growth and survival of a
community are submerged in this moment of social inertia.
He had not the ability or the energy to overcome the seducer.
He employed a social laziness which caused him to go along
with things. This conformist attitude did not ask what would
be the outcome in the long run. Woman and man did eat the
'forbidden fruit' but didn't physically die. Rather the power
of sin begins to impinge on the community living.

34

The Nature of Discord

Both Adam and Eve now became conscious of their nakedness; so much so that they made clothes to cover themselves. We read elsewhere in the creation story that 'both of them were naked, the man and his wife, but they felt no shame in front of each other' (Gen. 2:25). Now they are ashamed. The serpent had promised them new understanding. There is no doubt that their eyes were opened but what is seen is not something positive, or something that built them up, but rather something deflating. Shame is the daughter of sin and guilt.

> Certain disorders of the mind have their sources in . . . conflict. They differ from mental diseases caused by injury or deficiency of the nervous tissue. They are what is called 'compromise formations', by-products of the conflict.[12]

We know from all of this that shame or guilt did not originally affect just the individual but the two together. This meant that they were ashamed in the presence of each other – community. Man and woman in community are paying dearly for their transgression. They are called before the Creator in a series of questions and answers. They have to account for their deeds (Gen. 3:8–24). Responsibility is here seen as paramount to keep the balance of order and freedom within any community. Personal preference is not seen as a substitute for responsibility.

The relationship which existed between Adam and Eve and the animal kingdom is also broken. In Chapter 2 of Genesis we see the definite place which the animals had in the world of humans by virtue of each being named (Gen.

2:18–21). Now discord exists also in the animal and vegetable kingdom (Gen. 3:14–19). This discord will result in a power struggle and domination. 'Your yearning shall be for your husband, yet he will lord it over you' (Gen. 3:16).

This verse has lots of implications, yet for this book I take it as signifying discord in relationships. From now on, when men and women live together, indeed when people live together, there will be a search for equal rights. Social interaction within community will revolve around the search for power. This power will not be available to everyone.

> Power is a particular kind of reciprocal interaction involving interpersonal control or manipulation. It involves a dominance–submission relationship . . . whether or not this relationship is intentionally sought by the persons involved . . . Power includes all kinds of situations involving the ability of one person to influence or control the behaviour of another.[13]

Even a cursory glance at the world around us is sufficient to show that all is not well with community. When we go further, however, and enquire what is wrong, who is to blame and how it should be put right, then we receive a barrage of answers. For Christianity, the split in community exists from sin which led to division. This consisted in the breaking of a unity: first of all the breaking of Adam and Eve's own unity with God and then the weakening of the unity which would have bound them and their descendants together as a body. As a consequence this organic body lost its own internal unity, so that each person's passions and instincts – instead of linking together harmoniously for their welfare and God's glory – pull apart in several directions. It is precisely because of disobedience that community life is wounded. However, community life was not totally destroyed but had to be lived within a different corporate terrain.

A Covenant Community

A Searching Community

The Fall brought man and woman into a situation of moral autonomy on the one hand and estrangement and alienation on the other. Community was now in a condition of instability which would set in motion a cycle of events, some with disastrous historical consequences. Man and woman are forced to leave the garden (Gen 3:23–4). The existence of human beings now is such that men and women are forced to confront themselves and each other in a place from which God is apparently absent. They seem abandoned by God. Before God expels them both from the garden, he makes garments for them and clothes them. God is still concerned and paradoxically still accepts humans even in their fallen state.

The intention of this book is not to create a debate between Christianity and scientific anthropology, but rather to place community within its historical perspective. If community – whose very nature is historic – is to be changed, then it is necessary to work through a process whereby it is turned from itself and towards God for meaning. Moreover, since community is corrupted, then it makes sense that any transformation cannot come about by self-imposing powers but must rather come from a movement on God's part. This process of reconciliation and renewal is brought into history by the expulsion from the Garden of Eden and the transmission of discord to all human beings.

> As a result of the Fall sin has become universal; except for Jesus Christ no person who ever lived on this earth has been free from sin. This sad fact is acknowledged even by those who are neither adherents of Christianity nor believers in the Bible. The recognition that there is something wrong with the moral nature of man is found in all religions . . . the Koran, the sacred book of Islam, admits the universal sinfulness of man, understanding this sinfulness as being a violation of the will of a personal God.[1]

The Old Testament demonstrates God rebuilding community. It is not possible to trace the course of this rebuilding in detail; nevertheless I am dealing with the most important stages. Our interest focuses, then, on that particular segment of history which became Israel.

A Searching God
The faith of the chosen people is based on the belief that God had played a part in the history of Israel and had chosen her for himself. Israel thought of God as an all-powerful and all-knowing Creator. This great God uses wind and storms and plagues to effect his purpose; he humiliates Pharaoh and employs the proud might of Assyria in order to bring about his will. He is present with Joseph in Egypt;

with Moses in the wilderness; with Jonah at sea. There is no place from which he is excluded and his glory is frequently mentioned.

Yahweh God is seen as compassionate and gracious, slow to anger and abundant in mercy and truth. 'To the Israelites he was known more for what He did than for what He was. Thus we find that verbs rather than abstract nouns are most often used . . . He loves, forgives, judges, redeems, and so on.'[2] The constancy of God's love is declared and he demands that this love be answered in loyalty.

A Searching Humanity

A vast gulf separates humans from God. If that gulf is bridged in fellowship, it is by God's grace, and this filled the Old Testament people with a sense of unspeakable privilege and awe. The dignity that humans have is theirs because God conferred it on them. This highest dignity is not something inalienable conferred on them in their humanity, but is something that is theirs so long as they accept the conditions that it entailed. Humans in the Old Testament are presented as superior to the animal creation and charged with the rule of the 'lower' creatures. However, it is rather in their potential community with God that their real dignity lies. They may have community with God, but only so long as their hearts are right with God and so long as they bow before God in worship and reflect the will of God in their lives.

It is in this spiritual communing with God that a real community building process is possible. This communing makes possible divine inspiration of humans. Men and women in the Old Testament are not seen as wholly other than God. Having said that, humans are frequently held to be a vehicle of divine revelation; this is never conceived of in physical terms. Men and women are never seen as physical revelations of God. The human body is perceived to be inhabited by something more than breath. Humans are spiritual beings. This spiritual side denotes a quality of personality. 'God, create a clean heart in me, put into me a new and constant spirit' (Ps. 51:10) is a cry not just of the spiritual but of the whole person.

In the Old Testament, men and women are endowed with moral freedom. This freedom can be used to comply with or resist the will of God. When people listened to the seductive voices that called them away from God then their acts were essentially their own (Gen. 3:1–7). The fundamental character of sin is seen in that it comes between people and God and isolates them from God. Yet sin is also seen as being committed against community. Clearly Cain sinned against Abel, and David against Uriah. Sin is seen as an offence against the community of which the sinner forms a part. By this sin the offender lowers the level of goodness in the community. Hence, instead of being guided and sustained by community the offender becomes like a cancer in defiling it. So the Old Testament portrays a searching people – a people searching for God and searching for a bond of unity that will hold them together. The eager yearning of Yahweh is for the restoration of community, and his desire is to remove all barriers which Old Testament people have erected.

Individual versus Community

Faith is virtually nothing if it does not impinge upon the person as an individual. There is limited use in any debate about faith or conversion if it operates with little reference to the person. 'Faith of any persuasion involves some form of "conversion". It belongs to its very nature that it calls for response to God's presence in history, for personal commitment and human participation.'[3] However, there is a lack of substance in any debate if it is solely confined to the isolated individual or the recesses of their consciousness. Men and women are social beings and it is inconceivable that the faith dimension of their experience should not be important. Regardless of the truth embodied in the doctrine that faith has something to do with what the individual does in their own solitariness, the fact remains that the existence of a faith community is the most pervasive truth we encounter in the history of the world. 'The Community is obviously a social fact, one with which almost everyone is acquainted and yet it is one that few understand.'[4]

Hermits and solitary ascetics, reformers and prophets have existed but these figures stand out against the background of communities of believers bound together in a common faith. In the community dimension there are, therefore, bonds of understanding, purpose and devotion linking together many distinct individuals in such a way that their togetherness can be identified as an enduring whole or unity. Community itself is an ideal relationship based on the loyal acknowledgment of a common framework for interpreting human life; a common faith, common hopes and common tasks to be performed in the service of God.

It should not be strange to us then, that the Old Testament people were propelled by what is best called a sense of 'corporate identity'. Yahweh was the God of Israel and only secondarily the God of the individual Israelite. Individual faith existed, but it was construed through the community to which the individual belonged. In other words the relationship of the person to God, like the relationship of God to the person, was mediated through the corporate personality of the nation. 'Yahweh has taken Israel to belong to himself "the people of his own possession" . . . A community which is holy . . . that is to say set apart, separated from other people.'[5]

Meanwhile the prophets stressed in no uncertain terms the responsibility of the individual. The prophet Jeremiah makes the most notable contribution to the principle of individuality. He does this in the first place by the intensity of his own individual relationship with Yahweh, at a time when the national relation seems in imminent peril of dissolution. But his personal attitude becomes more explicit in the prophecy of the new covenant which Yahweh will make with individual Israelites.

Deep within them I will plant my Law, writing it on their hearts. Then I will be their God and they shall be my people. There will be no further need for neighbour to try to teach neighbour, or brother to say to brother, 'Learn to know Yahweh!' No, they will all know me. (Jer. 31: 33–4)

This prophecy seems to be set in opposition to the warnings that were given to Israel as a whole. The principle of individual responsibility is argued here. This is an important development in the focus of individual life. Here the individual is being summoned to take decisions which were bound to change their whole life. Jeremiah is hoping in this context that out of the profound convictions and decisions of the individual a code of conduct can be arrived at. This will have weaker connections with the ideals of a national community. Here a confrontation between the individual and community takes place. A new encounter with God is discovered and it incorporates humans into a new direct relationship with him. This thoroughgoing personalism of the new relationship between humans and God transforms the spiritual rebirth of the individual member of the nation of Israel. The preaching of Jeremiah and Ezekiel led to the shaping of an individuality which was to be the kernel of a new community.

> Jeremiah disclosed to us . . . truthfulness, courage, a hatred of the moral unworthy, an acute sensitivity, a warm humanity, and a serene confidence in God's purpose for the future . . . this does not mean an individualistic religion in which man is self contained in God. It is within the convenant (community) with Israel.[6]

But it could not be said that in the life of Israel we find neither extreme collectivism nor extreme individualism but merely a combination of both. The Old Testament writers believed that the life of every individual concerned the whole community, but they nevertheless saw the individual as an individual and denounced the sins of individuals as well as of society, and proclaimed the wrong suffered by individuals. There was a balance and a wholeness in their thought that is often lacking in our society. We think of sin as an individual thing. We also forget that our community has a life and a character and a will; and it may defy the will of God, to its own grave hurt and to that of its members. The Old Testament leaders recognised that people have sociality as well as individuality and that the community as well as the individual has a relationship with God.

The Bible teaches us a wonderful lesson in indicating to us that when a small minority repents then the whole nation is spared (Amos 5:15). A community that is rotten through and through may bring disaster upon itself and in some cases its corrupting influence spreads more widely. But where there is hope of reform even from a single person then divine mercy prevails (Jonah 3:6–10). Yet it is true to say that frequently individual people are involved in the disasters the unrighteous bring upon the community to which they belong. Good and bad are members of a common community. That a single individual may involve the whole community in disaster is amply emphasised by history. It only takes one traitor to betray an army or a nation, and a single careless deed may expose large numbers of people to danger. An 'evil' person is a social liability. If there is disease in the body at any point then it is a real menace until it is diagnosed by a doctor and removed. 'That is why I am going to lure her and lead her out into the wilderness and speak to her heart' (Hos. 2:14).

Leadership in Community

The last few years have seen in our society many great scandals, both in the political and religious spheres. These have all helped to undermine the role of leadership both in the Church and in the world. Where the individual is a leader of the community, it is not surprising that their acts do affect the welfare of the whole body. If a leader's acts are not in conformity with the office that they hold then that leader becomes a public liability. In the Old Testament there were no thoughts of the machinery of modern democracy. They had just the knowledge that if they walked in the ways of God then he would watch over them and send them the right leaders. 'I will give you shepherds after my own heart, and these shall feed you on knowledge and discretion' (Jer. 3:15).

However, it has to be said that where indifference to the will of God runs through a people it will have leaders who will lead it in an alien way. No matter how good the leadership, the spirit of an unbelieving community will suck them in and nullify their impact.

> When the people saw that Moses was a long time before coming down the mountain, they gathered round Aaron [Leader] and said to him, 'Come, make us a god to go at the head of us . . . a calf . . . Aaron built an altar before the effigy. (Exod. 32: 1–5).

The decisions and actions of a leader may involve the community in disaster or blessing. The private sin of David as leader of the nation necessarily came between him and God. When David was in a state of sin then this made it difficult for him to legislate for the wellbeing of his people either as individuals or collectively. He who is not at one with God will find it difficult to know his guidance. David, who repudiated the will of God in his private life, found it then difficult with sincerity to seek that same will in his public acts. It is clear, therefore, that when we examine the Old Testament we see that the corporate spirit of the community and righteousness of the leaders are both vital to strength and growth. The leader is a source of strength or weakness to the community depending on their own lifestyle. The life of a leader belongs to all, and the life of all around them determines their potential.

> Indeed it is difficult to distinguish leadership from
> kindred concepts like power and authority, not least
> because people in leadership positions typically exert
> (or at least have the capacity to exert) power and
> authority over their immediate subordinates.[7]

Among others, Jeremiah was a good leader. In Jeremiah 1:5 the Lord says, 'I have appointed you as prophet to the nations.' Among other things this surely means that God is exhorting Jeremiah to declare his will for that time to the nations, not least Israel itself. Jeremiah, from the outset, must have been well informed about the practicalities and history of his time. He was also aware of what was happening around him. He addressed the issue of the forthcoming invasion of the Babylonians from the north.[8] He warned other nations not to resist the Babylonians at the peril of being overrun themselves (Jer. 27: 1–11). He prophesied that the exile would last for three generations (Jer. 25:11). The service that this great leader shows us in his public utterances is the true concern for God's purposes for the nation of Israel and by deduction the application of God's purposes for all peoples and nations.

This leader is presented to us as overwhelmingly God's man. His life consists in coming to terms with the Word of God, finding ways to articulate it to his contemporaries, and living with the hazardous consequences of that reality. Such positive leaders were set at odds with their contemporaries. The call to leadership gave them an angle on historical reality which left them at times anguished, dismayed, depressed, yet hopeful. Their discernment of their day under the rule of God caused them to dismiss much that was valued and to discern in hope possibilities where their contemporaries saw none. The gap that existed between Yahweh and his people, Israel, is a combative distance and these good leaders do not paper over the cracks. They have a communion with Yahweh on the one hand while on the other they are subject to and involved in the day-to-day crises of the people. These good leaders are portrayed as having a good spiritual life but yet they are public people, preoccupied with public events, responsive to them and convinced that these public events are the ways in which Yahweh is having a say with his community. The constant theme that occurs in the Old Testament literature is one that talks of 'tearing up, planting and building'. These articulate God's decisive judgment and his resilient hope.

In the 'little book of consolation' (Jeremiah 30–31) the announcement is made that Yahweh has created something new to signify the new age into which a sorrowing despairing . . . [community] is invited to enter.[9]

A Covenant Community

The basis of the nation of Israel's existence is the particular relationship which exists between herself and Yahweh. This relationship is made from the earliest days in the form of a covenant. This covenant relationship is essentially two-sided. The Old Testament community was not just a nation bound to the land by a law, much like many modern states, but rather owing a common allegiance to Yahweh. This did not mean that they employed a spiritual arrogance in being a superbly devout or religious nation. It rather declared their faith that, through no merit of their own, they stood in a particular relationship to Yahweh; a relationship which is expressed in the word 'covenant'. A covenant is a relationship entered into by two parties, whether individuals or communities; an agreement implying rights and responsibilities on both sides.

One of the clearest examples of a covenant is the narrative in Genesis 31:43–54. The background to this story is a tale of mutual trickery and deceit between Jacob and Laban which resulted in Jacob's flight from his father-in-law's house. When Laban eventually overtakes Jacob, instead of further quarrelling which might later involve the shedding of blood he says: 'Come now, let us make a covenant, you and I . . . and let it serve as a witness between us' (Gen. 31:44). A mound of stones is erected to mark the spot where the covenant is solemnised and the contracting parties share a sacrificial meal as a sign of their new brotherhood. Any violation of this covenant will be avenged by God who witnessed it.

A similar story is told of the covenant between Jonathan and David which bound them together in friendship that only death could break (1 Sam. 18:3). The same understanding of covenant is employed to express the notion of covenant between Yahweh and Israel. In Genesis 15: 1–21 we see Abraham, in a moment of crisis, crying out to God. God then makes a covenant with him. Certain animals had to be cut in half to seal the covenant. In Jeremiah we read, 'And these men who have infringed my covenant [will be treated like the animals] they cut in two' (Jer. 34:18). This is the pledge for those who break the covenant. There are obviously serious obligations resting upon the covenant. It is God's covenant and it is a visible mark of the relationship which he established with the nation. For the community to survive it needed stringent guidelines. The tablets of the Ten Commandments at Sinai are seen as the charter of the covenant.

> The Decalogue is set apart from the other laws which follow. All Israel's laws were from God but the Decalogue had a special place . . . The Decalogue provides the basis for the Covenant with all of Israel.[10]

This covenant is seen as a declaration of the kingship of Yahweh over the nation. His style of kingship is one of liberator. He is the liberator who leads the people out of Egypt and enslavement into a new union which now claims their allegiance. As in the Genesis account of his dealings with Adam and Eve, Yahweh again puts responsibility upon his people. This is a community which is holy to Yahweh. One could ask, what led Yahweh to deliver this group of slaves from captivity and then enter into a covenant bond with them? The answer is love and mercy.

> God is the Lord: He has entered into a special relationship with His people, called a Covenant, and Lord is His Covenant name; He has revealed His special name to us and stamped our lives with it, as a sign of the love he extends to us and the response he requires.[11]

In the story of the covenant, the individual and the collective nation are committed exclusively to Yahweh. Their God was to be their one and only God.

> There is no other god besides me, a God of integrity

and a saviour; there is none apart from me. Turn to me
and be saved, all the ends of the earth, for I am God
unrivalled. (Isa. 45:21–2)

The word 'unrivalled' indicates the intense love of Yahweh
that had an exclusive bent on maintaining an exclusive claim
on his community. As well as the ethical breaking of the
covenant, it wasn't long before the people of Israel
apostatised in their faith. In the new land of Canaan the
people of the covenant found the native population
practising another religion. The future of God's community
lay not in the eradication or extermination of other people's
gods but rather in their own witness to Yahweh which
shunned compromise and continually disturbed the conscience of Israel. Surely we have a pattern here for Christian
living today. Rather than vociferously denouncing 'foreign
gods', we need to experience Christianity being lived
prophetically in a pagan society. 'A community where all
life is inspired and directed by the Spirit of Jesus Christ and
is lived to His glory [is] a witness and testimony to the
world.'[12]

There must have existed a terrifying possibility that God
might himself break the covenant. Nevertheless, their trust
in Yahweh's promise of community as solemnly declared in
the making of the covenant was so strong that it did not
allow their feelings to suffer any lasting sense of insecurity.
They were convinced that God was using this means to
achieve his purpose in history. Yahweh would not allow his
part of the covenant to be broken or violated, however great
Israel's unfaithfulness might be. This was their constant
hope.

A Community Built on Hope

The prophets of Israel were anything but optimists with regard to the immediate future. On the contrary, they attacked the religious, social and moral abuses of which their nation was guilty. They also criticised, in the strongest possible terms, the policies of the state and frequently declared that the nation was under the judgment of God and faced disaster. But their message of judgment was not their last word. They looked beyond the judgments they were compelled to announce, to a future when God would come again to his people in mercy, restoring their fortunes and establishing his rule over them in righteousness and peace. This promise of God's goodness is one of the most distinctive features in the preaching of the prophets and probably more than anything else served to bind the community of Israel together.

> By radically undercutting all facile claims on God's mercy and all false confidence in human merit, Ezekiel laid the sure foundation for the future hope of his people: God's sovereign freedom to cleanse and restore them as He saw fit.[13]

But with the post-exilic prophets there emerged an anticipation of divine intervention through which God would first bring judgment upon his people and then in the future deliver them and restore them, bringing his purposes for them to a triumphant conclusion. An example of this is when Hosea looks beyond the judgment for the renewal of the covenant blessings.

> That is why I am going to lure her and lead her out

into the wilderness and speak to her heart . . . I will betroth you to myself with faithfulness, and you will come to know Yahweh. (Hos. 2:14,22)

But where did this hope for the future come from? How is it that Israel, above all the other nations of her day, retained an unabated hope? One could be sure that the pagan states around them also had hope. This hope could have been purely for better times, for victory, plenty or peace. Surely these are attributes of hope that belong to all people. Israel experienced many reversals and maybe this provided an impetus for the development of hope. The confidence that the future was secure in the promises of God had therefore left a remarkable openness to the future. This hope was not just aligned to any rhythm of nature, the production of the soil or to the great achievements in battle or the spoils of war; rather it was the community's relationship to its God. This gave the nation a reason to exist. We know from the Bible how God called Abraham and promised him 'a land flowing with milk and honey'. We know that his descendants then went down to Egypt and were enslaved there. God liberated them and gave them a covenant relationship and laws to make them into a nation. All of these stories together with many more are the fulfilment of hope.

Perhaps the clearest example of Israel's hope lies in the account of the covenant ceremony at Shechem (Josh. 24: 1–28). Here hope is assured because of a realised past. Joshua gives an historical account of what God has done down through the ages, and on that basis challenges the people to respond to the renewal of the covenant. Israel entered history as a covenant society. Back with Adam and Eve there existed a sacred unity which is a focal point for hope.

> If . . . Israel's understanding of her God and her relationship to Him and position under Him . . . [is as profound as I describe above] it must have awakened in her a remarkable openness toward the future [and to hope].[14]

Therefore the Old Testament writers produce a defusing of despair, and emphasise the eternal origin and destiny of the individual and society.

> The biblical stories speak of the spirit of hope which is placed in God and which therefore even in the midst of nothingness puts its trust in the power of *'Creator ex Nihilo'*.[15]

4

Jesus and Community

A Community of Twelve[1]

I was so impressed when I went to visit the Taizé Community a few years ago. In understanding the community's underlying vision one needs to be familiar with the community's founder and prior, Brother Roger. It was Brother Roger's idea that brought the community into being and through his perseverance it has grown to its present-day size. In the Church today we have springing up large numbers of communities which are broadly based on the ideas and visions of their founders.

Jesus also founded a little community which gives us a blueprint of what our communities are called to be. Jesus's place in society is presented in varying ways from a timid, meek and mild man to a total superhuman of gigantic stature. While not intending to negate any of these suppositions I wish, in this chapter, to highlight the call that Jesus made to his disciples and in particular to the apostles to leave what they were doing and follow him. It is very clear that from the outset Jesus was not going to use angels to minister to people but rather his whole strategy was placed into the hands of human beings. Anything that had to be built would emanate from people.

The calling of the Twelve is extremely significant because it clarifies for all of us the intention of Jesus to lay the government of his Father's kingdom firmly upon the shoulders of ordinary men. He would, therefore, build a body of consecrated men in order to proclaim the kingdom. There doesn't seem to have been any haste in the choosing of these men. It seems from the Scriptures that he thought very carefully about what he was doing. 'As he was walking by the Sea of Galilee he saw two brothers . . . Peter, and . . . Andrew; they were making a cast in the lake with their net' (Matt. 4:18). This passage would seem to suggest that Jesus watched these men at work. A process of assessment and evaluation was taking place so that he could decide how efficient they were. He wanted the right men for the job ahead. His 'interviewing system' was based on observation – on-the-job assessment.

The twelve apostles were drawn from a cross-section of society. We see Peter who was impulsive and impetuous living in community with Judas, the avaricious one. It is interesting to note that none of the men summoned by Jesus held prominent positions in the Jewish synagogue. They were basically ordinary people who were not terrible well educated. Often they found the most elementary teaching beyond them and would turn to Jesus saying 'explain the parable to us' (Matt. 13:36). Yet they were called by him for the special purpose of preaching the gospel, which meant that they had to leave certain things behind and be prepared to embrace a future of inevitable uncertainty.

The impact that Jesus made upon these men must have been colossal. It appears that they were deeply moved by the initial experience of being called by Jesus. Nathanael, for example, after a moment's hesitation is overpowered by the presence of Jesus and proclaims, 'Rabbi, you are the Son of God, you are the King of Israel' (John 1:49). This new apostle makes a profession of faith in Jesus who is not, however, satisfied with it. He promises that: 'You will see greater things than that . . . You will see heaven laid open and, above the Son of Man, the angels of God ascending and descending' (John 1:50–1).

Jesus is a community builder. As we have seen in the Old Testament, the initiative is always on the side of God. However, this God has now become a human being. The mission and message of Jesus are the fulfilment of the will of God which led him along the path of the suffering Son of Man. He called these men to follow him along this way. This was the risk and responsibility which the community of Jesus found difficult to accept. He stayed close to them, faithful to them in their failures, believing that he was preparing this community of twelve for future encounters with the power of God.

A Small Community

In *Small is Beautiful*, E.F. Schumacher maintains the smaller the group the better the product.[2] Although Jesus concentrated on his small band of twelve, he did not neglect the mass of people, but rather, in the building of this smaller community, he would give the necessary impetus to the early Christian community to build the wider body of the Church. People join groups for almost every conceivable purpose: to make decisions, to solve problems, to satisfy social needs. Jesus's group of twelve came together because God was at its centre. Yet it could also be said that Jesus was the greatest psychologist[3] because he had an intimate understanding of human nature and therefore knew the best way to bind this little community together. It is obvious that much human behaviour takes place in groups. Governments conduct their business in small groups in order to improve the quality of decision making and productivity. Education employs small group discussion to facilitate learning. People form groups in order to plan social action. The community built around Jesus was made up of individuals who committed themselves to the group with their experience, knowledge and emotions. They brought to the group their energy and potential and in return must have shared the benefits of community living. One of the most fundamental needs of all human beings is to be affiliated to others. When such affiliation takes place formation can begin but a group cannot 'form' until its members have some shared experience.

> A small group is defined as any number of persons engaged in interaction with one another in a single face to face meeting . . . in which each member receives some impression or perception of each other member distinct enough so that he can . . . give some reaction to each of the others as an individual person.[4]

The identification as being part of Jesus's group would have occurred when the group had gone through a round of dealing with the anxiety of each member about their commitment as against the attractiveness of other things; and about the degree to which the group would influence their behaviour and present them with opportunities to be liked and to like. There is no doubt that Jesus sparked enthusiasm in the Twelve. The message they were receiving was revolutionary and would certainly have influenced their behaviour. The seeds of a costly discipleship were being sown. 'You have learnt how it was said: *You must not commit adultery*. But I say to this you: if a man looks at a woman lustfully, he has already committed adultery . . . in his heart' (Matt. 5:27–8).

Unity had to be created which took time – three years in fact. The group of twelve were being moulded to proclaim the kingdom, and this was not an open-ended community with new members constantly coming and going. If that had been the case then there would have existed a precarious balance of changing personnel who would have redefined the purpose and the day-to-day living of the group. Because this community of men formed a clearly visible boundary in its numerical make-up, then a considerable amount of time must have been spent with each other (Mark 4:10–12).

They were brought into a much closer interrelationship than would be the case in ordinary society. This would presuppose a cohesiveness far above that of rabbinical schools of the day.[5] This cohesiveness would have influenced a wide range of activities but perhaps its most significant influence would have been on the group itself. Friendship, co-operation and interpersonal reaction must have exerted strong influences upon members of the group to behave in accordance with the group's expectations. We may assume that each of the Twelve was attracted to Jesus and to each other, and therefore wanted the group to succeed.

A Community in Formation

Learning is so deeply ingrained in us that it is almost involuntary. Our specialisation as a species is an aptitude to learn. Other species begin their learning afresh each generation but human beings are born into a culture specialising in the conservation and transmitting of past learning. This means that humans cannot depend upon a casual process of learning but must be educated. The first thing that Jesus asked of the Twelve was that they be teachable. 'Like the clay that is pliable in the hand of the potter they, too, were going to be moulded by Jesus into the preachers of the Kingdom.'[6]

The life to which Jesus called them was not merely an austere and uncomfortable existence from which they could not escape. His teaching was seen by the Twelve to be a description of the life that they were already living. When Jesus said, 'Set your hearts on his kingdom first, and on his righteousness, and all these other things will be given you as well' (Matt. 6:33) he was not telling them about something that might happen in the future; he was reminding them of what they already possessed. When Peter stated that 'We have left everything and followed you' Jesus replied by pointing out what they had gained 'now in this present time' (Mark 10:28–30). They had already received a hundredfold for everything that they had given up. They had given up their boats, their possessions, even the full-time attachment to their families but had entered into the enjoyment of a relationship in which they lacked nothing. 'When I sent you out without purse or haversack or sandals, were you short of anything?' (Luke 22:35). They had to reply, 'No'.

The learning process of the life with Jesus brought self-denial but it also brought enjoyment. It was not something to be endured for a time because something 'better' was going to follow; rather it was the way in which they learned that 'eternal life' is now as well as in the future. In the Garden of Gethsemane Jesus said:

> Do you think that I cannot appeal to my Father who would promptly send more than twelve legions of angels to my defence? But then, how would the scriptures be fulfilled that say this is the way it must be? (Matt. 26:53–4)

He must have been trying to impress upon them that the life they were living was the life he had chosen and not merely an existence dictated by circumstances.

It is clear that the Twelve felt that they themselves could have planned things more effectively.

> Then Peter spoke to Jesus. 'Lord,' he said, 'it is wonderful for us to be here; if you wish, I will make three tents here, one for you, one for Moses, and one for Elijah.' (Matt. 17:4)

They were waiting for Jesus to begin his work but instead he involved them in his ministry (John 1:35–51). Jesus took them with him wherever he went, as we see in the episode of the feeding of the five thousand. He very quickly lets them know that the multitudes are as much their business as his. He asks Philip how they are going to feed them (John 6:1–15). When he sent them out two by two they learned the practical application of what he had taught them; the meaning of the life they had lived together. It was in this way that they would understand his teaching and he rejoiced with them.

> Yes, I have given you power to tread underfoot serpents and scorpions and the whole strength of the enemy;

nothing shall ever hurt you. Yet do not rejoice that the spirits submit to you; rejoice rather that your names are written in heaven. (Luke 10:19–20)

In the first period of his ministry up to the feeding of the five thousand it is not easy to distinguish between Jesus speaking to the mass of the people, to the body of the disciples, or to the Twelve alone. It is likely however that his teaching was generally given in public but later expounded and expanded to the Twelve (Mark 4:13–20). They had the means to understand, the ears to listen and presumably the conviction to take it in. They found meaning in it as they did things together.

Effective learning is less likely to come from without, from knowledge transmitted in a teacher-pupil format. It is more likely to follow from members' willingness to engage in shared learning to resolve difficulties felt by them to be real. It is more likely to follow from a willingness to participate in a process of discovery and enquiry in which members contribute their own experiences, offer their ideas to a shared learning process.[7]

It would be only after the resurrection when they would go back over it all that they would see the real significance of Jesus's teaching. At this first stage in community they were learning by just being together and sharing their lives together. It is highly unlikely that they realised the full extent of their formation and training, but their expressed ambitions and their questions are a sure sign that formation was taking place. They were adjusting their minds and their actions from an individual perspective to one of participation in community. It cannot have been easy for them to live this intimate, shared lifestyle and the strain of this new life led to power struggles, jealousy and ambition for which they were gently rebuked.

> James and John, the sons of Zebedee, approached [Jesus] 'Master,' they said to him 'we want you to do us a favour . . . Allow us to sit one at your right hand and the other at your left in your glory.' When the other ten heard this they were indignant . . . Jesus called them to him and said, 'You know that among the pagans . . . their great men make their authority felt. This is not to happen among you.' (Mark 10:35–7; Matt. 20:24–6)

Such manifestations should not surprise us and were a sign that they were learning. What should perhaps surprise us is the fact that none of them appears to have had a nervous breakdown. At least the Scriptures do not indicate that any of them were in bad health.

The experience that I personally have of living in community is favourable, but it is not easy. I share with people who have come from all kinds of different backgrounds and possess differing personalities. The blending together of these factors takes some getting used to. However, life in my own community is not really possible without trust and harmony. This takes time and effort to build.

John the Baptist had taught his followers how to pray, so one of the disciples came to Jesus and said, 'Teach us to pray' (Luke 11:1). Because of their background the Twelve would have been accustomed to pray but they obviously felt that this new way of life demanded a new sort of prayer.

They frequently saw Jesus depart to pray on his own but this was not enough for them. It is interesting to note that only towards the end of his life did Jesus allow them to hear him pray (John 17). He did not begin their training by pushing a devotional spirituality upon them which they could not have taken on board. Only as they absorbed his training into their daily lives were they able to undertake a life of prayer, and the prayer he gave them in the 'Our Father' tied in closely with the needs and expectations of their lives. Basically he was teaching them how to live.

There are many communities and churches today which emphasis teaching and the imparting of knowledge but very few who integrate this into a whole programme of formation. Rather their particular teaching is frequently used to distinguish them from other branches of the Christian Church to whom they may feel called to 'spread the good news'. A lot of these groups tend to work within a fairly closed organisation of thought which would stress the teaching of a particular way of life and even a particular set of beliefs. Their evangelism then is merely a declaration of encouragement to join their particular group, whereas the Twelve were formed in order to be of service to the entire world.

There is great danger in an overemphasis on the personal nature of salvation to the extent that we can fall into the sin of individualism which results in a 'me' and 'Jesus' syndrome that ignores the centrality of relationship between Christians and the world. To counteract this we need greater emphasis upon *formation* which is much more time consuming than the mere imparting of knowledge.

We face a crisis of community . . . today. Lack of

community testifies partly to a lack of [community] in the Church and partly to the individualism of Western culture and partly to the influence of broader social currents . . . but if the Church is to consist of communities of loving defiance in a sinful world then it must pay more attention to the quality of its fellowship.[8]

The Twelve were not separated by Jesus from their surroundings. They lived and worked in the world. But the life to which they were called was nonetheless different from what they had known before. Its uniqueness is perhaps best manifested in Jesus's attitude to the family. Peter, as we know, was married, yet at the request of Jesus he 'left everything and followed him' (Luke 5:11). Jesus spoke strongly about the permanence of the relationship between husband and wife.

Have you not read that the creator from the beginning *made them male and female* and that he said: *This is why a man must leave father and mother, and cling to his wife, and the two become one body*? (Matt. 19:5)

and yet he could say: 'If any man comes to me without hating his father, mother, wife, children, brothers, sisters, yes and his own life too, he cannot be my disciple' (Luke 14:26).

If we hear a contradiction in this then the Twelve must have been similarly puzzled. Jesus was saying revolutionary things about the life he wished his disciples to follow and giving them a new understanding of family life. In peasant society the basic relationship was father to son. Therefore the reason for marriage was to ensure continuity through the procreation of a son. Jesus switches this around by saying that the basic unit is now man and woman; husband and wife. He puts marriage in a new light and uses the Genesis story to reinforce his argument. This is the beginning of a new commandment that people should love one another, and in proclaiming this teaching Jesus is looking towards a society of equality which would put husband and wife on an equal footing.

A Community Commitment

Commitment, it seems, depends upon two elements. It presupposes certain beliefs and also involves a personal dedication to the action implied by these beliefs. Each element cannot occur without the other, but if someone is truly committed both elements will be present. An individual's commitment determines the nature of their lifestyle and few would doubt that the call of Jesus to his disciples contained an insistence upon commitment. It was going to be costly to follow Jesus. He was looking for the men who could give their whole lives and his community was to be based upon loyalty.

We see this manifested in the call of Matthew. 'As Jesus was walking on from there he saw a man named Matthew sitting by the customs house, and he said to him, 'Follow me'. And he got up and followed him' (Matt. 9:9). Matthew was a tax-collector and no class was more hated in the ancient world. The tax-collector was not only barred from acting as a witness in court or serving as a judge, he was even debarred from worship. Repentance itself was regarded as well nigh impossible for the tax collector. They were unjust in that they fiddled their takings to make a handsome profit. Matthew's 'office' must have been close to where Jesus was preaching and something in the invitation of Jesus must have gone straight to his heart. A more unlikely man to be an apostle would be impossible to imagine. Unlike most of the others, who were fishermen, Matthew was no foreigner to figures. However, the band of apostles were loyal to Matthew despite his profession. People would have said that never was there more unpromising material that Matthew but, in the hands of Jesus, Matthew became a missionary for the new faith.

It is interesting to note that Jesus did not run after people if they were not capable of commitment. We see this in the case of the wealthy young man in the Gospel who was too rich and possessive to give his riches away. Jesus 'looked . . . at him and loved him' as he walked away (Mark 10:17–22). How could Jesus build community with half-hearted people? One of the great tragedies of today's secular society is its lack of commitment, with the result that we become trapped in selfishness and individualism.

> Costly . . . [commitment] is the treasure hidden in the field: for the sake of it man will gladly go and sell all that he has. It is the pearl of great price to buy what the merchant will sell . . . it is the call of Jesus Christ at which the disciple leaves his nets and follows Him.[9]

Jesus and Community – Accident or Intention

Jesus was concerned with community because he called the Twelve and looked after them. But the question does arise, did he really intend to form community? Obviously he did address individuals; he did insist that each individual decide in freedom and constantly re-evaluate whatever decisions were made. Jesus was not just concerned for the individual but for the community too. In Mark's Gospel we see Jesus recognising the disciples as lacking in spiritual insight and being hard of understanding. The Twelve receive instruction on revelation which is not normally communicated to the crowds. Our concern here is not the content of that instruction which relates to the person of Jesus, his mission and discipleship, but rather that Jesus is setting aside a 'special' community by intent and sharing special knowledge with them.

There are a number of occasions when Jesus goes alone with the apostles (Mark 6:30–1). 'When he was alone, the Twelve . . . asked what the parables meant. He told them, "The secret of the kingdom of God is given to you" ' (Mark 4:10–11). Here a clear distinction is drawn between teaching given to the group of twelve and to the crowds. The Twelve as a community thus possess special knowledge which separates them from those who do not belong. It is important to note that this special knowledge is never given to individuals but always to a group, sometimes the disciples, sometimes the Twelve. The knowledge, therefore, belongs to community and not just to individuals. Sometimes Peter, James and John are the only apostles present with Jesus (for example, Mark 5:37–43), yet they are encouraged to share this with the wider community after the resurrection: 'As they came down from the mountain he warned them to tell no one . . . until after the Son of Man had risen from the dead' (Mark 9:9).

We know that shared knowledge unifies a group and serves to differentiate it from those who do not possess this knowledge. It also creates a danger that the group will become insular and arrogant. It is possible that it will seek a privileged position for itself and refuse to expand. Jesus addresses this danger in Mark 9:38–40: 'John said to him, "Master, we saw a man who is not one of us casting out devils in your name; and because he was not one of us we tried to stop him." But Jesus said, "You must not stop him." ' Rigidity may exclude people who God wants to use. The community Jesus formed can only remain healthy and grow by giving him to others. It can only exist while it continues to enlarge the circle of those who wish to share the life of God in Jesus.

A Community and Leadership

The fact that Jesus was committed to the Twelve is a truism. He had a close personal relationship with them. Good leadership cannot function in isolation. The body of the Twelve was a loving, caring and supportive one. This commitment to relationships was paramount in Jesus's life. However, it is clear that he tested their abilities and aptitudes as well (Matt. 10). No doubt innate abilities play a part in the scope and nature of our achievements. But what any one of us can do is directly related to our social environment and in particular whether we are living in a climate of appreciation, discouragement or indifference. Our ability to learn is not just a question of our intelligence but also whether or not we like the teacher and even more important whether the teacher likes us. Personal encouragement is most successful in raising our levels of achievement.

'Encouragement has been described as a basic requirement for any . . . approach . . . . An encouraging attitude . . . should be as all-pervasive as kindness and warmth.'[10] Most people need encouragement and one can assume that the apostles were no different. It is clear that Jesus rejoiced with them in Luke 10:17 where we are told that they 'came back rejoicing'.

As a leader, Jesus gave and commanded respect. Our experience tells us that a successful leader must be person-orientated and task-related. Surely Jesus was a master of both of these. The New Testament knew only one leader and that is Jesus Christ. There is, therefore, no successor to Jesus Christ nor could we think of anyone filling his shoes, yet it has to be said that Jesus clearly did want the Twelve to exercise leadership. When he had ascended it is obvious that the early community needed a leader. The centre of gravity among the Church is the enduring life of Jesus Christ. Authority and leadership exist within the body as all its members exist within the body. The Twelve have a distinct position in the Gospels. They moved and acted in close proximity to Jesus. It is upon the Twelve, primarily, that duty of the mission lies; the duty of proclaiming, of witness and of baptising.

Peter had a special position among the Twelve, as the Twelve had a special position within the whole group of disciples. A review of the theological implications of the primacy of Peter and its relationship to the Pope would take us far beyond the subject matter of this study. The position of Peter cannot just be understood in terms of the mission of proclamation. His position is also as leader of the Twelve. Peter does not receive his position from the early community nor does the early community receive its reality from Peter. The reality of this early community and the leadership of Peter go together. Peter is the one who is mentioned more frequently than the others. He speaks more often than the others and sometimes speaks for them. ' "But you," he said "who do you say I am?" Then Simon Peter spoke up, "You are the Christ," he said' (Matt. 16:17).

One could argue that these facts do not establish the position of leadership for Peter among the Twelve. Jesus changed Peter's name from Simon but that could be argued to be insignificant. All of the Gospels except Mark contain some kind of commission given to Peter. Peter's leadership leaves no ambiguity in the Jerusalem community as described in the book of the Acts of the Apostles. It is clear, however debatable, that the main objective in Jesus's mind was to create leadership and not leave the early community in chaos. He wished to delegate power and leadership.

What is needed in our communities and churches today is delegation. Delegation is not easy. It requires courage, patience and skill. It is one of the most important areas of a leader's job; for what they choose to delegate, to whom and at what stage is almost entirely at the leader's own discretion. Delegation is not the same as 'giving people work to do'. A leader delegates when they deliberately choose to give a subordinate authority a piece of work which the leader could have decided to keep and carry out themself. Successful delegation demands giving someone the responsibility and the power to action these tasks. Delegation thus involves a calculated risk, but it does wonders for the morale of any group. 'It is not the Lord's intention that any individual should carry a burden too heavy to bear. His intention is that the load of . . . concern, community care . . . should be shared.'[11]

As well as delegating, Jesus also shows us the need to create and train new leaders. Leadership in all walks of life is inevitable. Leadership may reside in President Clinton, John Major or Pope John Paul II. Leaders may be strong, they may be weak, they may manipulate, persuade or guide

– but they cannot be ignored or suppressed. Whenever people live or work together there will be leadership and fortunately or unfortunately the destiny of nations, churches and communities depends in a large part upon the kind of leadership they have.

I think that there is a tendency sometimes in Christian circles to wait for Providence to send us the right leaders. We need a process which will make a firm beginning in the deliberate development of the sort of leadership which can satisfy our real needs of calling a world away from selfishness and individualism and into community. I realise to some extent that leaders are born, not made, but nevertheless we need to anoint and appoint the right leaders and then train them. Leadership can be enhanced by training. Good leadership cannot be accomplished solely by having the potential leader read and hear lectures about leadership. Actual experience is essential. Potential alone is not enough.

> The (Christian) leader must steadfastly create a confidence in the future for a church and a people who are experiencing crisis ... leaders must develop insight and resilience so that mature human development is fostered in themselves and in others.[12]

The Fledgling Communities

Throughout the Bible, God reveals himself as community, acting with people he has chosen. The theme of God's involvement with certain communities runs from one end of the Bible to the other and if we try to remove it we have no Bible left. Those concerned are chosen not to be God's pets but to be his servants, that he may bless all people through them. First there is the nation of Israel. When the nation breaks its covenant it is cast into captivity but a chosen remnant remains. When this remnant fails to produce the goods, God sends his own Son. Jesus then gathers about him a new remnant – the Twelve – and the disciples. Thus far God's chosen people have all come from the Jewish community; after the death and resurrection of Jesus a new community of God's people comes into existence.

After the resurrection appearances ceased, the question uppermost in the minds of the early disciples must have been, 'has he vanished for ever, making no real change in the order of things?' With the ascension, it would have been thought that he had certainly vanished from sight. Just after the final commission in Acts 1:8, 'But you will receive power when the Holy Spirit comes on you, then you will be my witnesses not only in Jerusalem but . . . indeed to the ends of the earth' Jesus is lifted up and a cloud, the symbol of all that is mysterious, takes him out of sight. Chapter 1 of the Acts of the Apostles provides us with some details of the life of this fledgling community between the ascension and the day of Pentecost. We are told that they assembled together in the upper room and perhaps we wonder whether this may have been the same upper room in which Jesus ate the last supper with the Twelve. These chosen twelve, reduced now by the death of Judas to eleven, formed the nucleus of this little band of believers.

At the risk of safety and reputation, a group of about 120 came together following the ascension. Their chief occupation was prayer. Jesus had spoken of the promise of the Father, so until that promise came true they could only wait.

During his ministry Jesus was followed by a varying number of disciples, sometimes large and sometimes small. From among them he chose the Twelve 'to be his companions and to be sent out to preach' (Mark 3:14). We saw that it was not by accident that there were twelve of them. The most frequent name given to them is not 'the apostles' but simply 'the Twelve'. Now that there were only eleven, it was necessary for Judas to be replaced and the election of the twelfth man was preceded by a speech from Peter delivered to the whole company of about 120. This indicates that the new appointment was very important and also that it was of 'community' concern for those assembled rather than just a 'private' matter.

It is interesting to note that from the vast multitude who followed Jesus this band of 120 was all that was left. Yet from this 'small' gathering there grew in a single generation a Church that was to make its influence felt to the ends of the known world – Christians today should not, therefore, be discouraged by small numbers.

Peter concludes his speech by laying down the qualities necessary for the man who will take the place of Judas. He must be someone who has accompanied the apostles from the earliest times, as only such a person could be adequately equipped to be an apostle. 'Both the defection of Judas and the necessity of replacing him by someone more worthy are viewed as subjects of Old Testament prophecy.'[1] The new apostle is then chosen by lot, but the necessary qualifications and qualities would have excluded most of the 120. This is the only occasion in the New Testament when we see a leader chosen by lot. Perhaps the choice of the twelfth member in this way was necessary so that it could be seen as a direct appointment by the Lord; or possibly, after Pentecost, the guidance of the Holy Spirit was so clear as to make 'lots' unnecessary. In this sense, the unique apostolic witness could not be repeated. Through the substance of this witness and certain apostolic functions in the early Christian community, authentic teaching and practice could be handed on to others.

Pentecost Community

It would be difficult to exaggerate the importance which Luke, the author of Acts, attaches to the second chapter of that book which contains the account of Pentecost without which all the rest of our discussion on community would be meaningless. The source for this great event is set not in individualism but in community. The three major feasts of the Jewish year were the feast of Passover, the feast of Weeks and the feast of Tabernacles. Pentecost (the fiftieth day) is another name for the feast of Weeks and was held seven weeks after Passover. There was a bustling mass of pilgrims in Jerusalem and the little community of believers were still waiting for the Holy Spirit.

One of the most startling surprises here is that the Holy Spirit came upon them as a body. As well as the individual reception of the Holy Spirit, the collective community of believers is so important, in fact vital. The repeated emphasis on the fact that the Spirit was given to the whole group leaves us in no doubt about the importance that Luke gives to community. No believer here was elevated above another – the Spirit was poured out on the whole body and thus distributed to each individual in the fledgling community. Luke shows Jesus performing his ministry in the power of the Spirit: 'Jesus, with the power of the Spirit in him, returned to Galilee; and his reputation spread throughout the countryside' (Luke 4:14). But in Acts 2 we see the Holy Spirit given in a completely new way.

Until now the Spirit had been given to certain individuals or for particular events – for example in Genesis 1:2 'Now the earth was a formless void, there was darkness over the deep, and God's Spirit hovered over the water' – but not to a group of people. In the Old Testament, the Spirit was never poured out on all the people, only upon chosen leaders for a limited period of time. When the immediate crisis was over the Spirit departed.[2] These fleeting experiences increased the longing for this day of Pentecost when the Spirit would be completely and permanently bestowed. Moses cried out: 'If only the whole people of Yahweh were prophets, and Yahweh gave his Spirit to them all' (Num. 11:29). Joel longed for the day when the Spirit would be poured out not just on a few leaders, but upon the community. 'After this I will pour out my spirit on all mankind. Your sons and daughters shall prophesy, your old men shall dream dreams, and your young men see visions' (Joel 3:1).

On the day of Pentecost, these longings of the Old Testament were fulfilled. The Spirit came, not just to a few individuals during times of crisis but to dwell in the midst of the assembled community, to be the bond of that community, the secret source of their common life and the power for their mission to the world. This was followed by the great demonstration of the power of the Holy Spirit in community – they began to preach out of community and to invite others to respond to Jesus and come into community. It is recorded in Acts 2 that Peter's invitation was immediately accepted by some three thousand people. These new converts must have been gathered into that single-hearted enthusiasm which only the Holy Spirit can give. As a body they were caught up in a communal experience of ecstatic worship which manifested itself in visions. They recognised this as the impact of the Spirit of God in which they saw the hand of the risen Jesus drawing them into living community.

A Community of Hope
To trace the emerging self-consciousness of this early community is as impossible as the getting together of a biography of Jesus. As far as we can tell, the clear identity of the community seems to have developed from the experience of the Holy Spirit at Pentecost. The Holy Spirit gave them a communal enthusiasm and ecstasy which would have given this early community a sense of distinct communal identity. They were aware that their involvement in each other's lives came about through the Holy Spirit.

This sense of community was not therefore a mere sense of a shared experience, some sort of mutual admiration society, but rather the consciousness of a deep sharing of common life in a community of hope. What they had in common was far more important than anything that might divide them.

> The life of the primitive church . . . provides us with the most primitive account of the life and temper of the primitive Christian community . . . the church had its organised life under the guidance of the Apostles . . . The first uniting bond in the Church was the teaching of the Apostles.[3]

This first community of believers was still involved with the Jewish faith. Initially there was scarcely room for dissension between themselves and the pious Jews. They went to the Temple, and observed the common law. One point alone distinguished them. For them, the Messiah did not belong to a vague uncertain future – they had found him and were sure of certain things to come. The community grew rapidly and soon had to give up hope of incorporating itself into the main body of Judaism. There was opposition in Jerusalem where its lifestyle brought it into conflict with the religious authorities and public opinion. Opposed in Jerusalem, it spread in other directions.

The unity of this early community nevertheless has to be stressed. They remained locked in hope by two dominating factors. The community spread beyond Jerusalem remaining united in a common faith and single way of ordering their lives and worship. Whatever their differences of race, class and education they were bound together in a single loyalty, calling each other 'brother' and 'sister'.

> In this [community] the common people . . . found new
> life and new hope; they were no longer leaderless
> because if there was one thing more than anything else
> that was very real to . . . the community it was the
> presence and power of Jesus.[4]

One aspect of hope that we cannot deny in this early
community is their enthusiasm. An excitement gripped the
expectation of these earliest believers. Many of them were
disciples or apostles of Jesus – and they were filled with
yearning for his speedy return. The fact that the early
community shared a communal fund can be explained as a
natural expression of their enthusiasm as they waited for
the return of Jesus. It is highly unlikely that everybody
contributed substantially but presumably they all gave something. All this indicates a hopeful community rather than
the desire to establish a 'communist' state with communal
ownership.

These first Christians were not interested in the means of
production. In this first community their sharing was an
expression of love and mutual concern. Hope and enthusiasm gripped their community. They were almost lifted out
of themselves. Inspiration permeated the community which
gave them confidence and assurance.

Baptism is likely to have been a rite of initiation into the
community from the earliest days. The rite probably served
as an expression of repentance and would have been taken
over from John the Baptist with the difference that people
were now baptised in the name of Jesus (Acts 2:38; 8:16;
10:48). This is a clear sign that Jesus is the head of this
community which expressed its oneness in the breaking of

bread in the eucharistic meal which was eaten in different homes. To what extent these meals were thought of as sacramental is not at issue in this book. However, it can be argued that the words of institution,

> Take this, all of you, and eat it: this is my body which will be given up for you . . . Take this, all of you, and drink from it: this is the cup of my blood, the blood of the new and everlasting covenant. It will be shed for you and for all so that sins may be forgiven. Do this in memory of me

must have been recalled or used at some if not all of their community meals.

> The Jewish followers of Jesus continued to attend the temple . . . services, but as the breach between them and . . . religious leaders grew wider their own small community . . . [and the Eucharists] became a new centre of their religious life.[5]

The presence of the early community at this meal was a testimony to their new covenant status. The sharing of bread is a simple but important expression of themselves as community.

A Community of Worship

The worship of this earliest community centred largely around the Temple (Acts 2:46; 3:1; 5:12), but it is logical to assume that other forms of worship began to emerge as they met in one another's homes. It is possible that house gatherings predominated and those who met in this way would have been largely 'unchurched', which would have necessitated teaching (Acts 2:42; 5:42; 13:1). The greatest desire of their teachers would have been to expound the Scriptures and the words and example of Jesus. His sayings would have been repeated and the same stories about him would have been told to different groups of converts. If the object of teaching was to pass on the tradition, then biblical prophecy was used to transmit new revelations.

From the earliest days, we find a 'conserving' function (teaching) and a 'creating' function (prophecy) within the early community, with prayer as its most important feature. This involved the observance of the Jewish times of prayer (Acts 3:1) as well as participation in the prayer meetings of the community (Acts 6:4; 12:5). It can be assumed regular and spontaneous prayer took place in the different homes, revolving around thanksgiving and praise.

> For the praise of old psalms were used and new psalms composed. The prayers were in such a form that all could take part in their recitation. But Christian worship was not a precise copy of synagogue worship.[6]

The prayer of this early community finds its centre in Jesus as the focus of prayer. 'Paul and Silas were praying and singing God's praises' (Acts 16:25). Whether or not singing played a large part we do not know. Certainly the worship of this community was filled with heartfelt devotion (Acts 5:41; 8:39; 11:23) – this was more than just a good social get-together. It is obvious that their worship was inspired by the Holy Spirit and stemmed from a communal enthusiasm rather than tradition or hierarchy. It was an expression of their sense of community rather than its source.

Something drastic must surely happen to the Church today so that enthusiasm for community and worship may be resurrected. There is an accepted environment in the churches, accepted because it has become the norm. Many faithful people turn up to the announced services year in and year out. If they are bored, as many tell me they are, in private, they accept the responsibility of that upon themselves and don't blame the Church. 'There must be something wrong with me,' they tell me. There may well be something wrong with them; maybe they do need a new Pentecost in their lives, but yet they continue to go, to endure it, like some bitter medicine that must be good for them. It would be difficult to overestimate the damage done to the Christian faith over the last fifty years by the lethargy and apathy that we frequently find in our congregations. While we need people to speak out in radical discontent, we tend to discourage them because they unsettle and annoy us. But such voices may be the voice of God warning us against our lack of community and our lack of enthusiasm for the gospel.

> The 'sickness' of modern Christendom poses a problem. We need to make some searching self-diagnoses to examine our condition ... [The early Church] had its symptoms of malaise which were perhaps more its exuberance and enthusiasm ... than its lethargy and deadness.[7]

Worship and enthusiasm are the activities whereby a church builds up its members and expresses its community and nature. I realise that to think of worship and community without mission is to deal with an introverted church. To think of worship and mission without community is to make

Christianity an individualistic affair. We need to constantly ask therefore how our worship may more thoroughly partake of community; how we may express our togetherness, which mirrors the very being of God.

Community Lifestyle

The 'Born Again' movement throughout the world has emphasised – rightly – that salvation is a matter of personal relationship with God within an experience of conversion. 'Unless a man is born from above, he cannot see the kingdom of God' (John 3:3). However, there can be a great danger in an overemphasis on the personal nature of salvation. Salvation is *individual*, but this does not make it *individualistic*. Our salvation is a matter of coming into relationship with God and then into relationship with the body of Christ. By contrast, the attitude of many people, including 'born again' Christians, towards the community as part of Christianity is a reluctance to become too involved. When it is intimated that there is something more to being a Christian than our personal relationship with the Lord, we can feel threatened and wish to opt out. This is the expression of a model of Church which has more in common with the consumerist society than with traditional Christianity. The principal assumption today can be that the only thing that matters is for the individual to do whatever they want, and society elevates the self-made person as an example of someone deserving respect. 'But success is a tenuous business and theories about staying sane on this planet frequently need revising.'[8]

The life of faith, hope and love stands in direct contradiction to the values of consumerism. Faith, hope and love are the three human activities deemed to counteract the behavioural standards of a 'self' society. Lived belief, lived hope and lived love can only conflict with an atheistic society and need to be lived out in a communal life which fosters faith and enables the individual to live in a way that goes against the prevailing culture. Christian communities need to be formed which will call forth an individual fidelity of their members to a life of faith, mutual encouragement and hope; to an openness to share ministry in the light of that faith; to show hospitality and respect for all; to plan with respect the changes necessary in environmental conditions, and integrity within the larger body of the city or nation. In this way the life of a community stands prophetically against a consumer society.

If at community level faith, hope and love are purified as patterns of corporate life, then they will be able to bring greater compassion as well as insight into those areas which are found on a broader social and political scale. For this to happen it is necessary for a community to be visible. The Jerusalem community was very visible and impacted upon the culture of its day. This type of community was known as *'koinonia'* in the Acts of the Apostles. This was the solidarity of a common life and service of those called by God. The corporate nature of the gospel finds its expression in the coming together of this early community. This community is one unit and not just a collection of individuals. The Jerusalem community had solidarity with each other as members of one body with Christ as head and empowered by the Holy Spirit.

The *Koinonia* Community

Luke in the Acts (2:43–7; 4:32–5) gives us a general description of community life in the early Church. 'They would sell their property and possessions' (Acts 2:45 *Good News Bible*) 'and all that believed were together and had all things in common.'[9] They lived in this way for a considerable period of time. This common living of the early Church cannot be associated with Marxist communism, while on the other hand it was not a registered charity with its 'community chest'. It was a deep sharing among Christian brothers and sisters. It was a '*Koinonia*' community where the principal elements were not just a sharing in fellowship of worship but of responsibility for one another at every level.

> The Spirit-filled community exhibited a remarkable unanimity which expressed itself even in the attitude to private property. Each member regarded his private estate as being at the community's disposal.[10]

This type of communality was not unique in the first century. There were other groups who practised a community of goods,[11] but to enter them one had to turn all one's property over to the heads of the organisation. The sharing of wealth in the early Church was very different. Private property was not abolished. The people gave what was their own. To abolish private material things is to abolish giving, since a person can only give what they have. The sharing in the Jerusalem community was not forced but voluntary and was not a condition of entrance into the community. In short, the sharing of goods was simply the natural expression of a deep inner sharing in the Holy Spirit. Jesus had initiated some kind of sharing among the apostles, where Judas kept the common purse. Jesus suggested to the rich young man that he sell everything and give to the poor.

It was therefore only natural that the early Church should take Jesus's commands so literally. If one member of the community had more than they needed and a brother or sister was in want it would be unthinkable to hold on to what one had.

In Acts 5:1–11, the offence of Ananias and Sapphira is that they lied about the sale of their property. They were free not to sell but they tried to deceive the community. Later on in Acts we read that Peter visited the house of Mark's mother (12:12). It is clear from this passage that she had not sold her house and donated the proceeds to the common purse. The emphasis in the new community was on ensuring that all needs were met, on 'koinonia' of total belonging at all levels rather than merely at the institutional or organisational level. The phrase 'everything in common' must refer to a radical attitude of mind continually expressing itself in practical ways. When there was a need then some people really did sell their property and donate the proceeds to those in need.

It is understandable that, with the passing of time and the spreading of the community beyond Jerusalem, the enthusiasm for sharing should fade. Maybe this type of life was possible only for the Jerusalem community. With the spread of Christianity, its practical nature could not be deemed reasonable on a larger scale. Nevertheless, the spirit and motivation behind the sense of total belonging remained to some extent. The love that the Jerusalem community had for each other was alive. The care for one another was not only material or spiritual but it reached all spheres of life.

There is much evidence that the Church corresponded in deed as well as in word with the ideal of a community that cared for those in need. Writing in about AD 125 Aristides pointed out to the Emperor Hadrian that the Christian Church looked after strangers, provided for the burial of the poor, took food to Christians in prison and if necessary fasted in order to meet the needs of the poor and needy.[12]

The function of those early Christians was to act as members of a family or community. In our churches today we tend to distance ourselves from biblical principles by thinking of community as something to be taken seriously by those who like that sort of thing. It is possible for us to choose God as a 'private possession' without reference to our relationship with each other and the surrounding culture – accepting what is comfortable and ignoring the rest.

Community for Mission

The promise of being missioners is fulfilled for the first Christian community at Pentecost. The apostles and disciples are now given the same anointing which Jesus received at his baptism in the Jordan.[13] People of every nation are able to receive in their own language the good news of God. This is the gathering of the nations to be the new people of God in the new covenant.

Immediately after Pentecost, Peter stands up and preaches to the multitudes (Acts 2:14–36). One can reasonably assume that Peter's speech was made in the midst of his fellow believers and that he was therefore speaking from within the community. In fact there are up to twenty-four speeches in the book of Acts which accounts for roughly one-fifth of the book. Those sermons contain probably the best-known narratives in the book. Although preaching was not the only way in which the early Church missioned, nevertheless it is the basis from which the later Church developed. The missionary activity of the early Church represents the essential core of the Christian faith.

Peter stands amidst the others as a sign that he speaks for them all. Speaking out of the body of the community, Peter invites his listeners to become part of that body. 'Every one of you must be baptised' he announces (Acts 2:38). Baptism was the initiation ceremony into community. Peter's invitation is immediately accepted and, as we have seen, three thousand are 'added to their number'. In other words, the community was growing. Pentecost was the birthday of the Church, and saw the dawning of a new mission.

The new Church is launched, and the meeting between Peter and Cornelius is especially significant in that it throws light on the mission to pagans. At the beginning of this story we see Peter firmly rejecting what appears to be an assault on his fidelity to the old ways (Acts 10:9–16). His whole identity and indeed that of the community is associated with strong obedience to the laws of Israel. Despite his struggles, Peter is persuaded to go to the home of a pagan officer and share the gospel with him. The situation spirals out of control when Cornelius and his family start to experience the power of Pentecost. Peter knows that he is not in control because a power greater than his has broken down the barriers. He can only accept these pagans into the new community. This is clearly a community affair because Peter defends his action before the whole assembly. His final defence is, 'Who was I to stand in God's way?' (Acts 11:17).

It is made clear that in this story mission was changing the new community. There is conversion for the community as well as for Cornelius. It is not a matter of the community admitting a new person into its midst and closing the gates again. A community in mission is not just about church extension – something more costly is involved. Before the meeting of Peter and Cornelius, the Church was a society within the cultural world of Israel. It has now become a society spanning the divide between Jew and pagan. The community of apostles and disciples are witnesses to mission as long as they go where the Spirit leads.

The charity of the first community expressed itself in care of the poor, widows and orphans, prison-visiting and in social action during times of famine or war. Hospitality was exercised generously. Christianity appears to have made a strong appeal to women as well to slaves, on account of the teaching that all people were equal under God. Christian advocacy of the sanctity of marriage offered great security and it was frequently through wives that Christianity penetrated the upper classes and particular households. At the same time, Christianity cut across the ordinary social classes because it encouraged the idea of personal choice in freely joining this new community.

> The faithful all lived together and owned everything in common; they sold their goods and possessions and shared out the proceeds among themselves according to what each one needed ... Day by day the Lord added to their community. (Acts 2:44–7)

This was the experience of the community at Jerusalem. This community did not fit harmoniously into the structure of Israel, yet it exercised a strange attraction. The way of life was different and they used worldly things but did not put their trust in them.

Community or Church or Both

The letters of St Paul provide us with ample material for arriving at an idea of his thought and beliefs concerning the Church. The word '*ekklesia*', 'church', occurs about sixty times. Paul uses '*ekklesia*' to describe the body of believers. He speaks of the church of Cenchreae (Rom. 16:1) and the church of the Laodiceans (Col. 4:16). He speaks also of the churches at Galatia (1 Cor. 16:1; Gal. 1:1) and the churches of Macedonia (2 Cor. 8:1). He speaks of the care of all the churches which is upon his own heart (2 Cor. 11:28).

We know that in the infancy of the Church the gatherings of the early Christians must have been small. It was not until the third century that anything in the nature of church buildings came into being. In the early days, the believers were still meeting in houses which had rooms large enough to accommodate them. So Paul uses the word '*ekklesia*' for any part of the Church in any given place. However, '*ekklesia*' can be used as a description of the Christian community gathered in one place for worship and instruction. It can also be used for the company of believers in every place and in every nation. This community of believers is not to be regarded as a merely human organisation.

Twice Paul confesses that he persecuted the Church of God (1 Cor. 15:9; Gal. 1:13). In the two letters of St Paul to the Corinthians, there is a hint of the development of his thinking. These two letters are addressed to the Church of God which is at Corinth (1 Cor. 1:2; 2 Cor. 1:1). The Christian community is no longer the church of Corinth; it is the Church of God at Corinth. Here we see that the Church is not a collection of loosely integrated, isolated units. Two things may well have moved Paul's thinking in this direction. First, in Corinth he had to deal with great disunity. There were splits and fragmentation:

> From what Chloe's people have been telling me ... it is clear that there are serious differences among you ... all these slogans ... like 'I am for Paul', 'I am for Apollos', 'I am for Cephas'. (1 Col. 1:11–13)

Second, it may be that Paul's growing experience of the Roman Empire helped him in his thinking. A Roman colony was not a 'colony' in our sense of the term. Roman colonies were strategic centres which bound the empire together. These were composed of army veterans who had served their time and who had been granted citizenship. These colonies were little bits of Rome planted worldwide. The Church, in Paul's thinking, wherever its geographical location, is the Church of God. The idea of the unity of the Church took root in Paul's mind and developed. The concept of '*ekklesia*' was not a creation of the Christian community but has its roots in Jewish background.

> Yahweh gave me the two stone tablets inscribed by the finger of God, and all the words on them that Yahweh had spoken ... on the day of the Assembly [*ekklesia*]. (Deut. 9:10)

The new Israel (the Christian community) was no longer the nation of Israel; it was the Church.

Paul writes to the Christians at Rome and calls them

'brothers' (brethren) (Rom. 16:14). Herein lies the eternal truth about community. It is meant to be a family in which men and women are brothers and sisters. When a church is divided; when bitterness has invaded its ranks; when an unforgiving spirit has caused breaches which remain unhealed then that local church has ceased to be a real community. There is a common task within the body of Christ, namely to build each other up. Spiritual gifts are to be used for this purpose (1 Cor. 14:5, 12). Mutual upbuilding is the duty of the community members. 'So give encouragement to each other and keep strengthening one another, as you do already' (1 Thess. 5:11). Such a relationship implies a basic equality for all within the church. Paul writes of Philemon and himself as 'brothers' (Philem. 17). Paul uses the language of community and partnerships in virtually all of his letters. He suffers as a prisoner, and the Philippians participate in his comfort. They have a share in his troubles by giving themselves and their money (Phil. 4:10–20). This is a *'koinonia'* community because it is a mutual sharing in the blessings of the gospel.

6

The Pilgrims of Community

The 'Pentecost' community was soon to be scattered through persecution by Saul (Paul) of Tarsus and Herod Agrippa (Acts 9; 12). We do not know if the new communities continued to hold everything in common. They certainly encountered political harassment and there seems to have been little sympathy for them within the Roman Empire.[1] With the conversion of St Paul, an understanding of community seems to emerge which is at variance with that of the community in Jerusalem. In Ephesians 4:28 for example, Paul exhorts the new convert thieves to work with their hands so that they can save enough money to share with those in need. Here we find equality, justice and partnership as distinct from the clear-cut 'everything in common' (Acts 2:44). Was St Paul advocating individualism or merely tolerating a system that could not be changed? Certain things suggest the latter. Elsewhere, Paul is keen to encourage the rich to distribute for the good of their souls (1 Tim. 6:18) and he also gives a high priority to hospitality (Rom. 12:13). Elsewhere in the New Testament, Peter points out that false prophets who lead others astray will be characterised by greed (2 Pet. 2:13). The impression we receive is of a gradual lowering of standards and a more flexible orientation towards community.

From the writings of the early fathers at the close of the New Testament period, we can trace the development of Christian community. It seems that the lived experience of being and sharing was taken somewhat for granted in the early days, which enabled the fathers to concentrate in their writings on basic doctrinal errors. It is clear, however, that the lifestyle of the early Christians frequently ran counter to the world around them. 'Love' was the predominant factor in their lives.

> Let the rich man supply the wants of the poor, and let the poor man give thanks to God because he has given him someone to supply his needs.[2]

Justin Martyr and Tertullian, of the second and early third centuries, wrote that the early believers lived frugally but that on a given day they gave their surplus to the aged and infirm or to those suffering persecution.[3] Sharing was obviously the norm, but it would be naive to suggest that problems did not exist and the situation was extremely more complex. Groups led by charismatic and doctrinal leaders frequently broke away from the main body; Marcion, for example, formed his own community while Montanus, Novatian, Donatus and Arius[4] all claimed to be *the Church*.

These splinter communities varied in their criticism of tradition and doctrine, yet their protest was inevitably against the 'mother' community. Perhaps it is useful here to trace the history of certain different Christian traditions. The reader may not find their tradition or Church dealt with in this work. I hope, nevertheless, that I will be awarded the understanding of how impossible it would be to adequately deal with all branches of the Christian Church.

Roman Catholics and Community

The Catholic Church professes a tradition stretching back to the Church of the apostles and therefore believes itself to be deeply rooted in community.

With the conversion of the Emperor Constantine at the beginning of the fourth century, Christianity was again forced to reorientate itself. Until this time, the early Christian communities had found themselves to be frequently at odds with political systems and social behaviour. Constantine effectively introduced the principle of 'one society, one faith' which I consider to have been a retrograde step because it helped to blur the distinction drawn by Jesus between earthly kingdoms and the kingdom of God. If the lifestyle of Constantine and the leaders of the empire had been wholly admirable, these might have been less of a problem but their way of life was frequently indistinguishable from that of the pagans.

With the dawn of the Church/State merger, a further debasing of Christianity occurred. The call of Jesus to live in unity (John 17) had to be maintained in Christian teaching, but there were now severe limitations upon its practical application. Nevertheless, the call to community was not going to disappear and a solution was found whereby a truly communal life could be lived in a prophetic way by a smaller number. Thus the high ideal of a communal lifestyle for *all* is now reduced to the few. The great debate between the worldliness of individualism within the Church and the call to community became the unresolved tension.

Monasticism

As a means of avoiding the world altogether, men and women decided to withdraw to the desert in solitude to pray, fast and intercede with God for their brothers and sisters. The attraction of a life completely dedicated to God drew others to join the hermits and these formed small communities with everything shared in common. The 'desert fathers', as they came to be called, grew in number because of the Christian longing for community. Communities of men and women were separated, with celibacy seen as the most elevated path. The mingling of the sexes would be too much of a temptation. The communities drew up rules emphasising three essentials: poverty, chastity and obedience; in order to counteract the worldly influences of money, sex and power. They were centres of prayer, healing, hospitality, shelter and education.

> We have surrounded ourselves with the wall of salvation, which is love for the law of God and for the vocation to Koinonia that we might walk upon the earth according to the ways of the company of heaven . . . since we truly love one another.[5]

Outside community walls, the Church continued to call men and women into belonging but not to the radical commitment of the desert fathers. They were encouraged to share faith, prayer and possessions, retaining the right to private property.[6]

Several bishops began to live in community, sharing their lives and property with others. Among them was St Augustine of Hippo in north Africa, whose monastic rule advocated the complete sharing of possessions. His example was followed by others and the move towards monastic life gained momentum. St Basil, revered in the Orthodox Churches, lived in community and wrote at length about the need for Christian community life.[7] St Basil advocates that those who strive for the same goals should live a common lifestyle, and by the year 425 we know that the priests of the Diocese of Rhinecorurus in Egypt are living communally.[8] Throughout the so-called Dark Ages of the sixth, seventh and eighth centuries, the monastic life spread throughout Europe – St Patrick bringing the concept to Ireland.

St Benedict's monastery at Monte Cassino (*c*. 525 AD) was uncompromising in its emphasis on communal life. However, the joyful monasteries of St Augustine and Basil were soon to become institutionalised. Over the centuries, the monastic life continued to flourish despite a growing over-organisation. Meanwhile, the Church beyond the walls of the monasteries was becoming increasingly individualistic. By the eleventh and twelfth centuries, monasteries had been to some extent infected by the worldly emphasis on power and money and some form of renewal was necessary. Renewed fervour for the common life was introduced by the Cistercians at Citeaux, Clairvaux, Rievaulx and elsewhere.

The Community of Friars

The coming of the friars in the twelfth century brought tremendous impetus to the Catholic Church. These men lived in the world and did not withdraw from it like the monks. Friars were essentially preachers, living a common lifestyle but with a roving commission, originally combating heresy, ignorance and apathy. St Francis remains an inspiration to Christians and atheists alike, with his emphasis not only on self-denial but on a simplicity of lifestyle which attracted men and women from all walks of life, not least the outcast and marginalised.

Franciscans, Dominicans, Carmelites, Augustinians and others were soon making a great contribution to Christian communal life as well as to the wider community through their contribution to education and social services in the broadest sense. The friars rapidly achieved great popularity and made a considerable impact upon Europe. They were to play a leading role in the building of universities in the Middle Ages where men such as Roger Bacon, a pioneer of modern scientific discovery, owed their education to the friars. The friars were as effective as the monks of the earlier centuries in keeping alive the movement from individualism to community.

Side by side with monks and friars walked the 'third orders' composed of men and women who did not wish to enter monasteries or friaries but wished to be associated with the lifestyle of orders like the Franciscans or Dominicans. This was an indication that ordinary people were drawn to community and an indication that the Church was not catering for the ordinary individual. The community dimension of the gospel was believed to be a lived experience only for those in 'vows' but not for anybody else. The decay in the Catholic Church which led to the Reformation could be broadly attributed to the lack of true lived community.

The Catholic Reformation Communities

The great influence of Martin Luther in the sixteenth century was due not so much to his original thinking as to the fact that he spearheaded the growing criticism of the Church. He began not with a wholesale attack but rather with an exhortation to the Church to reform. Luther was followed by Zwingli, Calvin and others, and the Reformers took their stand upon the Bible, rather than the Pope. They gave 'personal faith' back to the ordinary man and woman. However, hand in hand with this personal faith was the danger of division and individualism, and before long the Protestant Reformers were breaking into different factions, each one claiming to have the 'true' interpretation of Christianity. Calvin, the 'thinking' father of the Reformation, based his model of community on the rigid Augustinian rules. This doctrinal split was soon followed by Henry VIII in England.

The Catholic Church responded to the split by creating new religious communities based broadly on strict obedience to the Pope – such as the Society of Jesus, with the emphasis on consolidation and the closing of ranks. The Jesuits founded by Ignatius Loyola became an outstanding Order, preaching and teaching against the Reformers. However, the concept of community was now seen in terms of reaction. Protestantism was perceived as individualistic and Catholicism became reactionary. The new Orders brought with them new standards of living, particularly in ethical life. The continuation of the founding of new religious Orders of men and women continued right up to the end of the nineteenth century. The emphasis moved slightly from that of being a consolatory Church to that of being a missionary Church, especially among the New and Third World countries. Among the most famous of these Orders was the Redemptorists, founded by Alphonsus Ligouri in the mid-1800s. At the beginning of the twentieth century, new Orders of priests and nuns appeared, dedicated to missionary work abroad, such as the Mill Hill Fathers and Sisters, the Columbans, Killtegan Fathers, and others.

Post-Vatican II Catholicism and Community

The Council called by Pope John XXIII in the early 1960s focused the Catholic Church upon mission and community. Although it is very early to write a historical evaluation of this call, yet it is still evident that there is a growing desire for community living among Catholics, with an increasing concern for social justice and the sharing of wealth. A number of communities have had a remarkable influence on the Catholic Church since Vatican II – such as the Focolare Movement, Marriage Encounter, charismatic communities and Basc Christian Cells – and a number of them have developed as a direct result of charismatic renewal.

These new neo-catechumenate communities highlight the need for spiritual renewal, love for one another, discipleship, teaching and training, and ethical living. These communities have a strong missionary impact because they endeavour to incarnate the gospel '*koinonia*'[9] and demonstrate genuine community sharing, equality of membership, love of Jesus and unity in a common cause. Thus Christian community is beginning to be perceived by Catholics as something essential to church faithfulness rather than an optional extra. Vatican II has shown us that community is not just necessary merely for sociological reasons but for fundamental spiritual ones, and that a Church without community is a Church without strength.[10]

Through her individual members and her whole Community the Church believes she can contribute greatly towards making the family of man and its history more human. In addition the Catholic Church gladly holds in high esteem the things which other Christian Churches or ecclesial communities have done or are doing co-operatively by way of achieving the same goal.[11]

Community and the Church of England

It is not easy to examine the extent to which community characterises the Church of England because the Anglican Communion contains three discernible historical strands: Catholic, liberal and evangelical, to which may be added the charismatic.

The Catholic Strand

The principal way in which the Catholic strand in Anglicanism has spread is through the sacraments. Baptism, as the once-for-all act of initiation, and the Eucharist are the sacraments of continuing relationship between Christ and his people. Both are essentially corporate, even though both involve the individual. It is the individual who is baptised and who partakes of the sacred elements. However, baptism cannot take place without sponsors who pledge the commitment of the candidate to the Church. Likewise, the Eucharist cannot be celebrated in isolation within the Anglican Church, as there must be at least two other people present to celebrate this communal meal with the priest.

The Catholic strand in Anglicanism is emphatically communal in other respects. It is unusual to find in Catholic circles a stirring challenge to repentance and faith, as regeneration is seen as having taken place at baptism, and the whole ethos of a Catholic Anglican church is essentially communal and sacramental.

> Faith was a gift, its source the Holy Spirit acting through the authoritative teaching of the Church, its medium the sacraments of the Church.[12]

There can, of course, be weaknesses as well as strengths in this approach. What if there is no faith, no response to the heavenly Lover, either at baptism or the Eucharist? What, indeed, of those who go through the motions, but do not believe it?

The Liberal Strand

The liberal strand in Anglicanism attempts to persuade people into faith, showing belief to be a reasonable enterprise and is, therefore, an individual undertaking. It may, of course, involve a small group but essentially the liberal strand attempts to enable people to see that although the gospel transcends reason it is not opposed to reason. Nowadays, the liberals in the Church of England are wary of attempting to evangelise anyone. They are respectful of people's private space. They are happy to dialogue, but are often unwilling to attempt to dislodge anyone from their beliefs or to assess and evaluate belief. A number of Anglican liberals are sceptics and have, like Don Cupitt (Dean of Emmanuel College, Cambridge), adopted a form of Buddhism, 'taking leave of God', or straightforward agnosticism. Here there is plenty of individualism.

> Though Anglicans acknowledge an authority in human reason, there appears in practice some uncertainty as to what this means . . . Did it lead on to holiness, unity and service?[13]

The Evangelical Strand

The third strand in Anglicanism is the evangelical. Enormously strengthened through the First and Second Awakenings in the eighteenth and nineteenth centuries, there has been a major resurgence in evangelical Christianity within the Anglican Communion, especially since the Second World War. This has partly resulted from Billy Graham's crusades; partly from the student work of the Universities and Colleges Christian Fellowship; the predominance of evangelical ordinands; and an interdenominational evangelicalism which has swept the world. The strength of this movement lies in its clear confidence in New Testament Christianity. It speaks to our hunger for certainties, is life-transforming, and brings many thousands of adult sceptics into Christian faith.

Evangelical Anglicanism does not see baptism alone as the guarantee of regeneration, but rather as its sacramental symbol and pledge. New birth comes when the Holy Spirit of Christ is received into one's heart and life – and that is something to which baptism points but which it cannot ensure. In addition to baptism with water in the name of the Trinity, full Christian initiation requires the human response of repentance and faith, and the divine gift of the Holy Spirit. Only then does the seed of new life germinate.

Most Anglican evangelicals emphasise that God's gifts are conditional on our response to them. This is challenging, but can be individualistic if the gospel is reduced to a divine promise to which only the thoughtful adult believer can respond. It is distressing that the evangelicals, who have been strongest in denouncing the Enlightenment, are themselves the most obvious heirs of the Enlightenment, and nowhere more so than in the rationalism which characterises them and the individualism which springs from Descartes' disastrous '*cogito ergo sum*'. The evangelicals, therefore, although by far the most enthusiastic Anglicans, particularly in this half-century, are in great danger of surrendering to the individualism which is the antithesis of community as depicted in the New Testament. And they are heirs to the Age of Reason, the most individualistic and indeed inherently atheistic intellectual regime to have been devised within the past three hundred years. If anyone is guilty of identifying evangelism with individualism within the Anglican fold, it is the evangelicals.

The Charismatic Strand

The charismatics are not easy to define – nor is that surprising since the Greek word '*charisma*' is applied in the New Testament both to something as natural as marriage and to something as all-embracing as eternal life. But this century has seen a remarkable flowering of Christians who emphasise the power and regenerating influence of the Holy Spirit. They have discovered that the most crucial element in Christian initiation is the work of the Holy Spirit, bringing us to a new life with God, and imbuing us with gifts to fulfil his calling.

The language employed has frequently been unfortunate. 'Baptism in or with the Holy Spirit' was once a key phrase of the movement, but people are coming to realise that the phrase is only used in the New Testament to describe an *initial* experience of the Spirit of God rather than a second state of initiation. Nevertheless, millions of Christians do experience a life-changing second awakening in their lives, often associated with the development of spiritual gifts such as speaking in tongues, healing, deliverance ministry or some aspect of prophecy. This is not necessarily an individual experience and many charismatics will tell you of spiritual gifts falling upon a whole roomful of people or of entire communities overwhelmed with an awareness of God and entrusting their lives to Christ as a result.

Unfortunately, in the West, the charismatic movement has degenerated into something happy and clappy, often with regrettable judgmentalism towards other Christians. At its best it is God's empowering for mission – and as such, is certainly not individualistic. It revels in the very super-naturalism discounted by the eighteenth-century Enlighten-ment which placed reason above faith. Now charismatics can, and do, go over the top. They are in great danger of confusing their own imaginations with the guidance which the Spirit can give. Nevertheless, they are a force – perhaps a third of all professing Christians – and are to be found in every Christian denomination. At their best, they embody the most effective evangelistic outreach in the Christian community.

> Their vision is to 'create an environment where people who have committed themselves to the Lord Jesus can work this out in a loving commitment to one another in such a way that the Holy Spirit can fully use His gifts in their lives'.[14]

Charismatic Christians have not, as a whole, resolved the dichotomy between community and individualism. It would be true to say that they run into danger of descending into individualism. This is tragic, because the New Testament models are so obviously corporate, and our society desperately needs a cohesive change of climate to be brought about by the Christian Church at large. However, efforts are being made to correct this.

> The Church is emphatically not an agglomeration of pious individuals who happen to believe ... All too often Christians talk about 'my Christian life, my faith, my salvation, my relationship with God' ... The Church is also a community of sinners ... called to be saints, but ... perhaps increasingly aware that we are a fellowship.[15]

Evangelicals and Community

Every year, several thousand people visit Lee Abbey – one of the oldest and best-known of the evangelical communities in the United Kingdom which exist 'for the renewal and growth of the Church'. This summarises very well the major raison d'être for evangelical involvement with community, emphasising witness to Church and society rather than relationship. The three main strands within such witness are an apologetic or proclamatory role, providing a centre for ministry (usually healing), and a model of alternative community.

The Apologetic Role

Perhaps one of the earliest examples of evangelical community was that established in Germany in the 1930s by Dietrich Bonhoeffer to enable men to live together in the spirit of genuine brotherhood while training for the ministry in what was then known as the 'confessing church'. Bonhoeffer was concerned to provide a true opportunity for Christian formation and teaching within the degenerate climate of Nazi Germany. One of the major features of evangelical community has been the provision of sound teaching alongside a training in the Christian virtues; reflecting the evangelical commitment to proclaim the good news of the life-changing love of Christ to the individual. The goal has always been the transformation of the individual in order to enable them to be an influence for good, rather than the extention of community. The main thrust of witness is the desire to 'go out and tell' rather than to be 'in relationship'. Consequently, whether we examine the recent 'Men's Movement' in the United States, or the conference centres such as Lee Abbey and Scargill House in the United Kingdom, or the rapid growth of the house churches also known as new churches around the world, the involvement in community is a comparatively brief experience of preparation for the main aim which is to go out and tell others of Christ.

A Centre for Ministry

Within the last twenty-five years, there has been an explosion of Christian healing centres within the evangelical world. These are task-orientated, having a central core of members who live in community in the belief that they have been called to offer care and ministry to others. Again the focus is largely upon the needs of the individual for healing and personal growth. Some, like the Maranatha Community in Northern Ireland, seek to address the unhealed wounds of both their own members and the county in which they are set. However, even this is largely through the trans- formation of the individual through conferences and meetings rather than networking into the strands of a fragmented society.

Yet we must make mention of a growing awareness in

such caring communities of a need to look at people in their life situations and provide a way of extending care into community structures. An example of this endeavour is the American Association of Pastoral Carers with their emphasis upon psychosystemic care. This means, in other words, that in order to care for the person we must also care for their world.

The Model of Alternative Community

In the 1960s, there was a proliferation of communities in which young people could try to live evangelically in an alternative way. The advent of the Jesus people in California represented a coming together of people concerned to address a number of issues. It was a youth movement, tired of conforming to the outworn lifestyles of a materialistic society, with a growing desire to reconnect with a God who is present to encourage and affirm the good rather than proclaim what is forbidden or unacceptable. It embodied a yearning to have meaningful encounter and dialogue in human relationships rather than just be taught what to believe. The Jesus People in California were largely a commentary upon the failures of modern society. They aimed to show a better way of belonging. To a large degree, this is also true of parallel communities, such as the Evangelical Sisterhood of Mary which began in post-war Germany in Darmstadt; the L'Abri Community in Switzerland founded by Edith and Francis Shaeffer; and the Sojourners Community founded by Jim Wallis in Washington DC. They attempt a lifestyle which conforms to biblical principles and seeks to comment upon such wide issues as reconciliation, ecology, art, justice and peace.

Over the past ten years, there has been an increasing

desire to widen and deepen spirituality, and the trend has been for evangelicals to look and learn from a more Catholic tradition in which relationships are the prime concern. Lee Abbey, in the West of England, has opened a number of homes in the industrial areas of the West Midlands of the United Kingdom where a small number of Christians live in prayer and fellowship which is itself a witness rather than proclamation. Many churches have adapted the structures of their liturgy and emphasise shared personal growth. Historically, one can see the influence of the musical, *Come Together*, which marked a point of departure for many evangelicals in the way they shaped their services with more time being given to sharing than to preaching or praying.

Another development has been the renewed interest in Celtic Christianity, with its emphasis upon integration between 'mother nature' and God's creation and the necessity for 'soul friending' with the community of two sharing their spiritual journey. Finally, we should note an increasing desire to belong to the wider community, and a growing recognition within the evangelical community that we are full members of our society with all its shortcomings; that true healing will come about through our taking our place within that society, rather than standing outside it offering correction.

The Christian Community Movement of the Late Twentieth Century

There have been three main surges in 'the quest for community' by Christian seekers, amongst others, during the twentieth century in the West.[16] Between the two world wars, reconciliation, the search for a new economic order spurred on by the Great Depression and the quest for peace (with the Society of Friends to the fore) were the main catalysts for action. Following the Second World War, a rather more sober and realistic mood launched a lower-key quest for a new educational and spiritual awakening, rooted in groups and fellowship of a more democratic bent.

The 1960s saw the most significant revival of the twentieth-century quest for community. This was triggered by the civil rights movement in the United States and Europe; by anti-war fever prompted by the existence of nuclear weapons, and the war in Vietnam; and by the questioning of power structures which seemed incapable of bringing about a better world. These forces coincided with a dynamic youth culture and vast improvements in technology. The Christian Churches were caught up in this climate of promise and protest, with Vatican II, the search for Christian unity and the radical theology of the 1960s reflecting the mood of change and challenge.

The Christian community movement of the 1960s emerged out of the maelstrom of this decade and reflected numerous features of the wider secular scene – the creation of communes to embrace or replace the nuclear family; concern for justice and peace issues; the search for a new unity of humankind beyond the old institutional divides; and the hope that 'an alternative society' was about to be born. The Corrymeela Community in Northern Ireland (1964), the Ashram Communities (1967), and the Blackheath Commune in South-east London (1969) were the forerunners of a veritable explosion of Christian groups and communities which took place in the early seventies and also regenerated established communities such as Iona, off the west coast of Scotland, and Lee Abbey. In 1971, the magazine *Community* was founded, and continues today as

Christian Community even though its circulation has rarely exceeded seven hundred.

The first gathering of new communities together with members of religious Orders (Anglican and Roman Catholic) took place in 1977 at Hengrave Hall in Suffolk, itself the home of a mixed community of 'religious' and 'lay' people. Out of this gathering came a commitment to meet and share resources more fully, leading to the establishment of a community resources centre in Birmingham in the same year. In 1980, the first Community Congress was held in Birmingham, attended by 250 people representing 106 'basic' groups (fifty-three residential groups or communities and fifty-three non-residential groups or networks) and forty-two religious Orders (thirteen Anglican and twenty-nine Roman Catholic). A year later, the Community Resources Centre for the National Association of Christian Communities and Networks (NACCAN) was established with a strong and representative steering committee.

The Christian community movement embraces a kaleidoscope of small groups and networks whose main interests range from living together to spiritual renewal, from education to a concern for the environment, from a service role in the fields of health and welfare to radical political issues. Some groups are tiny, and others – like the L'Arche Community (a community of men and women with learning difficulties) – have many houses. Some are relatively permanent, others disappeared in under twelve months, but 'community' is at the heart of their quest.

A second national Community Congress was held in Birmingham in 1984, and a third in 1987 although members and energy were beginning to ebb. The retrenchment of the seventies and especially the anti-communal ethos of the Thatcher years in Britain (1979–90) were taking their toll on the visionary community leaders of the sixties, but the Christian strand within the wider community movement proved more tenacious than most.

In the late twentieth century, the Christian community movement has been criticised for being white and middle-class and has found it hard to communicate its vision of an alternative Church (and society) to local congregations. It has fallen foul, as a fundamentally ecumenical movement, of the denominational retrenchment which has taken place over recent decades. It remains an often forgotten movement in many of the churches of the world. It may yet, however, prove to have within it the seeds of renewal for our individualistic society and the Church of the twenty-first century.

Community – Protestant or Catholic

Catholicism and orthodox Protestantism have differed greatly from one another, yet both have laid great stress upon the Christian faith as the ultimate truth. Catholicism has always emphasised the Church as the guardian of the truth. As St Paul says:

> I am hoping that I may be with you soon; but in case I should be delayed, I wanted you to know how people ought to behave in God's family – that is, in the Church of the living God, which upholds the truth and keeps it safe. (1 Tim. 3:14–15)

Protestantism has laid emphasis upon the biblical message, and rightly so because it is the Word of God. 'Take great care about what you do and what you teach; always do this, and in this way you will save both yourself and those who listen to you' (1 Tim. 4:16).

Yet deep differences are still perceived to exist between Catholics and Protestants, and the first step towards true ecumenism must be the acknowledgement that at present

Christianity is tragically divided. Common ground certainly exists despite our differences, yet we cannot romanticise or sentimentalise this imperfect unity. Papering over cracks or putting plasters on to broken limbs are not acts of real love. To live out the unity which is Christ's will (John 17:21) we must not only *acknowledge* the pain of divided Christianity but actually *experience* this pain. In a broken world, a broken Church is crippled in its witness to the reconciliation and wholeness offered in Christ, so any sign of rapprochement based on truth is to be welcomed. One area where this is possible is that of community.

> We share in Christ's anointing only as we share in His body, in the baptism wherein we die we die with Him and are raised with Him, and in the common life wherein by the manifold gifts of the Spirit the body is build up in love and furnished with all that it needs for . . . mission.[1]

This is an area where the different traditions can learn from each other to their mutual benefit and ultimately to assist in the preaching of the gospel to a world which needs so desperately to hear it. First of all, we must be clear about terms. Even terms which we take for granted can be understood differently. So first we must ask, what do we mean by 'Catholic' and 'Protestant'?

'Catholic' and 'Protestant'
When presented with terms such as 'Catholic' and 'Protestant', one can imagine two different systems, clearly defined and distinguished, suspiciously facing each other over a deep crevasse. This is a profound misunderstanding

and one which must be put aside before any discussion can be fruitful. This book is written from a Roman Catholic perspective but this does not excuse me from seeking to understand others and hoping that others will understand me. So, before we can engage in our search we must come to terms with the self-understanding of our own and others' churches.

To some people, Catholicism is clearly defined. Perhaps popular images such as the Pope kneeling to kiss the tarmac of another airport or the imposing dome of St Peter's in Rome are immediately identified as symbols of Catholicism. To others it may be mantillas and rosaries, while to others clerical collars and mitres. But these do not define Catholicism. Even the term '*Roman* Catholic' does not delineate the boundaries of the Catholic Church. Besides the churches of the Roman (or 'Latin') rite there are other churches in communion with the Bishop of Rome. The Ukrainian rite Catholic Church is an example of this. And outside the direct authority of Rome one could say that the Orthodox Churches stand in the Catholic tradition. Even within some of the Churches of the Reformation one will find Christians who consider themselves Catholic. The 'High' Anglicans, or 'Anglo-Catholics', are a clear example of this. This broad Catholicism has a distinct understanding of community.

If in Catholicism we find breadth then in Protestantism we find a veritable array. Perhaps in some ways 'Protestant' is not a particularly informative word. Historically, it was a derogatory rather than descriptive term. It began to be used in the aftermath of the Second Diet of Speyer in 1529 which sought to end the toleration of Lutheranism in Germany. As a response, six German princes and fourteen cities protested.

These people were disparagingly called 'Protestants'. From then on the term was basically synonymous with 'non-Catholic'. However, it was a catch-all term which really defined very little, considering the vast differences between say, Luther and Zwingli, or the magisterial Reformers in general and the radical Reformers, whom Luther called 'the fanatics'.[2]

Other 'Protestants' tended to call themselves 'evangelical', a term which was used especially in the 1520s to refer to those holding reforming views based upon a reading of the New Testament 'evangel'. There are also those within the Catholic Church today who hold beliefs which are 'evangelical'.[3] We will use the term 'Protestant' here to mean those non-Catholics of a broadly evangelical belief. Within Protestant evangelicalism there are many differences but also basic agreements on such matters as the material sufficiency of Scripture, the importance of a personal appropriation of faith and the priority of evangelism. Therefore the term can be used to describe a particular form of belief. Although amongst evangelicals there is a variety of approaches to community, there is nevertheless an underlying unity, as we shall see.

There is a growing awareness that it is possible to learn from other Christian traditions. Many Catholics today are finding, within evangelical Protestantism, elements and emphases consonant with a truly and fully Catholic Christianity, without feeling the need to deny their Catholicism. The reverse is also true, as many evangelicals recognise the riches in the historical tradition of the Catholic Church. In her deepest heart, the Catholic Church believes herself to be 'evangelical', rooted in God's revelation of himself in Jesus Christ, conveyed to us by his Word in

Scripture. 'All the preaching of the Church, as indeed the entire Christian religion, should be nourished and ruled by sacred Scripture.'[4]

At the same time, Protestantism believes itself to be a true expression of historic Catholic Christianity.[5] This is not to play with words or, like Humpty Dumpty in Alice's Wonderland, to have words mean whatever one wants them to mean. Rather, it demonstrates the depth of division which exists. The same words are often understood very differently. This does not mean that we should cease our longing for unity or our search to heal the rifts. It simply means that we should honestly seek to understand what other traditions hold dear and how this can complement a divergent understanding. This is what we are seeking to do here. Catholic and Protestant understandings of community are divergent. But perhaps they are also complementary. I shall examine the differences which exist, seek where possible to understand why these exist and then attempt an honest dialogue between the two.

The Unresolved Tension of Community in Catholicism and Protestantism

A glance at the theology and practices of the different churches could lead one to make sweeping generalisations and assumptions. These may involve some truth, but can be more a source of misunderstanding or misinterpretation. To understand a tradition properly one must understand, as far as possible, all that has gone to contribute to that tradition. Take a simple analogy: to fully understand a conversation I have wandered in upon I must know either the people who are conversing or the topic at hand. With this prior knowledge I can then interpret the experience I am having.

The same is true of so many areas of our lives. Our background and our past influence our interpretation of our present. To understand the discourse of both Catholicism and Protestantism on community one must know the history and influences which have aided in the construction of such views.

As with all doctrine, single items or themes cannot faithfully be examined in isolation from others without considerably lacking essential information and thus impairing judgment. A simple example would be seeking to understand the Trinity without any reference at all to the incarnation. This of course would be impossible. We must not fall into the trap of artificially dividing what is essentially linked. We must also recognise the limited scope of our own perspective. Often we take our experience, our time and our culture as definitive. We often assume that our own standpoint is objective. To understand Catholic and Protestant views of community we must lay aside prejudice, take time to examine the history involved and be ready to treat any relevant related issues.

A generalisation which has often been made is that Protestantism is individualistic and Catholicism is institutional. Although there may be truth in such assertions they are not complete. Perhaps we could more safely say that, in terms of the community, individual dialectic Catholicism tends towards the community and then works '*top-down*' to the individual whereas Protestantism tends towards the individual and then works '*bottom-up*' to community. To substantiate this understanding and seek out its implications I will look first at a Catholic view of community and then at a Protestant view before moving on to see what the two have to offer one another.

Community in Catholicism

In common with all Christians, Catholics see their roots in the people of Israel whom God called together to be his people. From being a nomadic tribe they became an established nation, a community worshipping God. Central to the Jewish notion of nationhood was community. Everything revolved around community. The worship was communal, focusing on the temple at Jerusalem. Feasts were celebrated communally, often as a family. One's identity was communally defined in terms of membership of a tribe and a family. Life was communal. The greatest sins were held to be so because they somehow affected the community. These sins were blasphemy, adultery and murder. All of these were sins against the community as well as against God. Blasphemy was a sin against the God who had formed Israel and held it in being. Adultery was a sin against marriage, the basic unit of society and community. Murder was a sin against the individual, who was a privileged member of the community of Israel. The community and God were seen as intimately linked through covenants. From the wanderings of Abraham, through the Exodus, to the establishing of the kingdom of Israel, the Old Testament is the story of God's formation of community. Throughout its pages the words echo: 'I will be your God and you shall be my people' (Lev. 26:12; Jer. 32:38; Ezek. 36:28; 37:27; 2 Cor. 6:16).

Christ came as the fulfilment of Israel (Matt. 5:17). He gathered around himself a community. He chose twelve men to symbolise the twelve tribes of Israel and so announce his purpose. As God led the twelve tribes so Jesus led the twelve apostles. He sat, he ate, he walked and he worked with his community. With his death, the community seemed shattered. But with his resurrection the community of the Church was gathered, empowered and sent forth.

Hence the Catholic Church's roots are profoundly communitarian. Seeing its foundations in Israel and the community of the New Testament, the Catholic Church has always stressed the priority of community. Monasticism in the first centuries and religious Orders subsequently have all been expressions of this emphasis upon the community. Reflecting the same emphasis are sodalities such as the Knights of St Columba, the Legion of Mary and the Catenians. The basic unit of Catholicism is community.

As the community of the new covenant founded by God, the Church has consistently been aware of the responsibility that this entails. Just as the promise was given to Israel not just for Israel's sake but for the sake of the whole world (Gen. 18:18; Ps. 71:11; Isa. 2:2; Jer. 3:17; Ezek. 36:23; Zech. 8:23) so the Church has been entrusted with the gospel not just for its own sake but for the sake of the whole world (Mark 16:15; Rom. 8:19–21). The Church thus understands herself to be in the form of a sacrament. She is the sign of truth and an instrument in the economy of salvation.[6] This must be briefly explained. The truth of the gospel message of salvation through the person of Jesus Christ, God incarnate, is not available to unaided human reason. Without specific revelation, humans may come to a vague knowledge of the existence of God (Rom. 1:19–20) but for saving knowledge God must reveal himself. People can only guess at what God is like but God himself can tell us for sure. He has done just this in his self-revelation in Jesus. This is the gospel. The disciples were charged with spreading this good news to all (as in Matt. 28:16–20). We can see that the gospel was proclaimed through the Church. The Church, therefore, believes herself to mediate the message of the gospel to the world.[7] This does not contradict the sole mediation of Christ as expressed in 1 Timothy 2:5 (NRSV):

> For there is one God; there is also one mediator between God and humankind, Christ Jesus, himself human, who gave himself a ransom for all.

Rather, it recognises that knowledge of Jesus is passed on through the Church. The Church asserts that even the most ardent fundamentalist, with a disdain for all things 'Romanish', actually possesses their knowledge of Christ through the proclamation of the Church. This will be an unsettling thought for some people, so I need to explain myself. No Christian is a Christian in complete isolation. Even if they should hold only to the plain words of Scripture, these very words were conveyed to them through history by the Church which safeguarded the Scriptures, making sure that they were conveyed intact to them today. Thus every single Christian stands in the line of tradition. The evangelical theologian, Richard Lints, writes:

> The message of Scripture is transmitted from genera-tion to generation in a variety of ways. It is handed down through a set of practices, a body of beliefs, and a cultural ethos. The theological use of the term tradition signifies the means of passing on the message of the Scriptures from generation to generation. In this sense, every theologian and every believer stand within a theological tradition.[8]

So the Catholic Church believes herself to be the minister of the gospel to the world.

An important factor in Catholic views on community is the idea of '*communion*'.[9] Communion is perhaps the central and defining feature of Catholicism. The gospel is seen in terms of communion with God. The Church is seen in terms of communion with each other. In Catholic thinking, the two are indistinguishable. The Church is part of the gospel. God always calls people into community. It is true that in the Bible he did call specific individuals, such as the prophets and apostles. However, these individuals were called for the sake of the community, be it Israel or the Church. Thus to a Catholic, communion with God is unthinkable without communion with each other. The community is therefore not just like a club or a society, but it is a communion of people who belong to each other. At its worst, this fades to a 'cultural Catholicism' where one is committed to the community without being committed to God, while at best it involves a sacrifice of one's whole self to the cause of the gospel.

At the Reformation, this understanding of the community of the Church came under threat. In response, the Catholic Church pulled up the drawbridges at the Council of Trent in 1546. From this time, the Catholic Church tended to become an insular counter-culture rather than a witnessing Christian community. The role of the Church as a counter-culture is seen in the way Catholics had separate schools, separate clubs; in effect a separate society. It was virtually possible to live one's whole life without contact with the non-Catholic world. This defensive mentality led to an emphasis on the community and Church to the detriment of the individual. The individual became a small part in a very big

Church. With Vatican II, this balance is being redressed. Many Catholic individuals are finding a freshness of personal faith which in turn nourishes community.

Therefore, in Catholicism the initial stress is on the community, which passes the faith on to individuals. The situation in Protestantism is quite different.

Community in Protestantism

The Reformation of the sixteenth century undeniably marked the splintering of Western Christendom. Much has been written on this and it would be safe to say that the period of the Reformation and the events surrounding it is probably *the* most extensively studied historical period.[10] From all this study, it is clear that the Reformation was not a movement insulated against the social and intellectual currents of its time. A brief, but by no means exhaustive, survey of some of these currents will be relevant here.

A new intellectual and social movement was growing towards the end of the fifteenth century. This time preceding the Reformation has now come to be called the Renaissance. This was a movement which touched on just about every area of life. One of its main elements of interest to us here is the particular movement which is now called 'Renaissance humanism'. This humanism had little to do with what we would think of as humanism today. In our time, humanism involves an atheistic emphasis on the person. Renaissance humanism was nothing of the sort. It was a search for spoken and written eloquence; an elegant simplicity and rhetoric which had been swamped by the logical rigour of the mediaeval scholastics. In the secular world this meant a revival of interest in the great Greek and Roman writers, while in theology the backdrop was the quest to return *ad fontes,* to the sources, of the Bible in the languages of Greek and Hebrew and the fathers of the first centuries. These were seen as far more reliable guides to Christian doctrine and practice than the mediaeval Church and the scholars with their fine philosophical distinctions. A leading light of this approach was Erasmus of Rotterdam. The movement advanced with the emergence of printing, and an increase in literacy. What had previously been the preserve of educated clerics and monks with their expensive hand-copied manuscripts was now available for examination by the laity. The 'person-in-the-pew' no longer had to accept statements at face value; they could now find out for themselves. There was thus a growing awareness of the individual as an individual.

The historian, Jacob Burckhardt,[11] has argued that it was at the Renaissance when human beings first began to think of themselves as *individuals*. The mediaeval world had been a world of communal consciousness, but with the Renaissance this gave way to a new awareness of individuals within society. The Renaissance was by no means a purely individualistic movement and the roots of its emphasis on the individual could be seen to go back to the fourteenth and fifteenth centuries. Nevertheless, the role of the individual as an independent agent was increasingly important. This new awareness of individuality brought new theological questions, particularly regarding the individual's stance before God. The Church had been seen as a mediator of salvation, ministering the sacraments and teachings about life. The popular view had been that one needed only to follow the appropriate teachings of the Church and there was no need to be worried. Now individuals did worry.

It is well documented that the impetus for Martin Luther's

reform was a fear for his own personal salvation. Although he was an academic, his search was personal. 'Where may I find a gracious God?' he asked. His experience was not unique. The young Italian, Gasparo Contarini (later a Catholic cardinal and the main Catholic representative at the Colloquy of Regensburg in 1541),[12] struggled in a similar way and had a conversion experience similar to Luther's. This happened earlier than the Saxon monk's. What is important is that the individual was emerging from the crowd and seeking assurance of their personal salvation. The tension between community and individual had once again raised its head.

The context in which the Reformation took place was a new awareness of the individual in their relationship to God. Lutheranism found its expression in the doctrine of justification by faith. In the Reformed Church, it found expression later as the doctrine of election or predestination. Lutheranism taught that the individual could indeed stand before God through the 'alien righteousness' of God given to him. Calvinism, which came to characterise Reformed theology, taught that the individual could stand before God in the knowledge that they were one of the chosen, the 'elect'. The individual could experience direct relationship with God, without need of mediation from any intermediate body such as the Church. Now the individual did not really need the community of faith, the Church.

Luther's initial dispute with mediaeval Catholicism was primarily doctrinal, while the dispute of the Reformed Church was concerned with the nature of the community, the Church itself. Luther did not intend to break with the Catholic Church. In 1519 (two years after the disputes surrounding his ninety-five theses) he wrote:

> If, unfortunately, there are things in Rome which cannot be improved, there is not – and cannot be – any reason for tearing oneself away from the Church in schism. Rather, the worse things become, the more one should help her and stand by her, for by schism and contempt nothing can be mended.[13]

This was indeed the thinking of Lutherans up until Regensburg (also known as 'Ratisbon') in 1541. They were now led to the sad conclusion that Rome could not be reformed. When Huldrych Zwingli began his reforming activities in Zurich he was perhaps more concerned with structure, discipline and liturgy than with specific doctrines. He asserted the authority of the local congregation over the wider Church and concerned himself with the affairs of this local church. His teaching contrasted greatly with that of Luther. Zwingli taught a doctrine of justification by moral regeneration, which amounted to justification by works, and his sacramental theology tended to see sacraments as mere expressions of community belonging.[14] Soon the two reformers were in dispute. However, at Marburg in 1529 a fair degree of unity was achieved between the two, and remaining differences were laid aside. The mainstream Reformers wanted one reformed Church. The Church was not to be discarded but reformed, and the reformation of the individual was seen as central to this.

The Reformers' emphasis on the individual within the Church is clear. However, it would be wrong to call the Reformers rampant individualists. The Reformed Church, in particular, held discipline and conformity within the Church to be essential. Bucer even made discipline a defining characteristic of a true church, alongside the preaching of the Word of God and the correct administration of the sacraments. Calvin did not go so far; he too stressed the need for unity, believing that there was no further need for division within the Reformed Church. Calvin held the community of the Church to be of divine institution. So, rather than glibly calling the Reformers individualists, it would perhaps be more accurate to say that they emphasised the need for personal conversion to God, direct relationship with him and subsequent fellowship within the community of the Church. Calvin even borrowed Cyprian of Carthage's two great ecclesiological maxims: 'You cannot have God as your father unless you have the church for your mother', and 'Outside the church there is no hope of remission of sins nor any salvation.'[15] The Reformers held the community to be important while stressing the centrality of the individual.

All of this is dealing with the magisterial Reformation. As far as the relationship between the individual and the community is concerned, the radical Reformers were very definite individualists. The Anabaptists held the Church to be a community made up *solely* of the redeemed. This was resurrecting the Donatist heresy of Augustine's time. Here the tension between the individual believer and the community was very definitely decided in favour of the individual. They believed that individuals could interpret Scripture for themselves, a belief which was quite different from the other Reformers' belief in the plain sense of Scripture. The magisterial Reformers retained an element of communal interpretation of Scripture, invoking tradition in favour of practices they did not feel were necessarily contrary to Scripture (such as infant baptism). This

Anabaptist tradition, with its emphasis on the individual *against* the Church, rather than *within* the Church, still exerts some influence today.

We can see that although the magisterial Reformers stressed the importance of individual faith, they did not overlook the importance of its communal expression. Throughout the history of Protestantism, the notion of community has been essential to its growth and strength. We can take three simple examples to illustrate this. When Calvin was embarking upon a programme of evangelisation in France, central to his approach were small 'cell' communities or '*églises plantées*'. These were really little more than religious study groups, whose members met for prayer, worship, Bible study and mutual support. Through these underground groups, 'agents' from Geneva were able to enter France to evangelise, unknown to the authorities. The groups grew quickly, proving attractive especially to those in the middle classes.[16] It would seem that a small group of committed individuals were able to exert a great influence on those around them and thus bring others into the group.

Similarly, when evangelicalism was beginning to assert itself within the Church of England in the eighteenth century, central to its flourishing were small groups or 'religious societies'. The members of these groups met for mutual upbuilding, committing themselves to regular attendance at Church of England services. A third example is provided by the Christian Unions set up in many universities, schools and colleges in the twentieth century by groups such as Scripture Union and the Inter-Varsity Fellowship (IVF, later known as the University and Colleges Christian Fellowship, UCCF). Again by meeting regularly for mutual support, prayer and Bible study, these groups helped to establish evangelical Christianity as an influential element in today's Church.

We can see that in Protestantism, far from dismissing the Church as irrelevant, the magisterial Reformers held the fellowship of the Church to be essential to Christian living. Some extreme Reformers (the Anabaptists) did discount the Church completely but this was certainly not the norm. Nevertheless, a change in understanding did take place. The Church came to be seen as essential to discipleship but not essential to the economy of salvation. Individuals as individuals need to come to a personal faith of their own. The Church, although 'mixed',[17] is thus essentially a *fellowship* of believers; that is, individual believers coming together without losing their individuality. This can be seen to contrast with the Catholic view of the Church. This view is that the Church is a *communion* of believers, each being interdependent and *belonging* together. This could explain why Catholics generally feel much more at home with the word 'community', while Protestantism frequently uses the word 'fellowship'.

A Comparison between Catholic and Protestant Views of Community

Catholicism and Protestantism hold in tension the balance between individual and community in the life of faith. Neither ignore this tension but they do approach it in different ways. The Catholic approach begins with the community. The community is the guardian of the faith, passing it on and sharing it with individuals who then appropriate it for themselves.

On the other hand, the Protestant approach to the balance

is quite different. It begins with the individual. The individual comes to faith without the mediation of the Church through the direct revelation of God as conveyed in Scripture. This individual then joins with other individuals of faith and fellowship is formed.

Both approaches will have criticisms of the other. The Catholic approach would perhaps accuse the Protestant of not appreciating the historical nature of salvation, which is entrusted to the body of believers who pass it on to the next generation. (Even the Scriptures, it is argued, were formed out of the body and are handed on intact by the body.) The Protestant approach would perhaps accuse the Catholic of interposing the Church between individuals and God in a way which is not necessary, since the Holy Spirit alone convicts, commits and leads to salvation. But we wish to see how each can benefit from the other's understanding, rather than going further into criticism. Ultimately, criticism reflects the particular emphases which different approaches hold dear. On identifying these emphases we can see how they complement one another and so gain a fruitful and complete understanding of the relation between the individual and the community.

Community and Spirituality

How one views community will inevitably affect one's spirituality. Louis Bouyer sums this up:

> Thus Protestantism tends to produce a spirituality which springs entirely from the co-presence and mutual relationship between the Person of God revealed in the Christ of the Gospels and the individual person of the believer. But, for Catholicism, there is

no fully authentic Christian spirituality without the realisation of an equal co-presence of our fellow-believers with Christ and ourselves, the Church.[18]

We can say that the Protestant emphasis is on *immediacy* and the Catholic emphasis is on *communion*.

The Protestant approach is one which puts the individual as the 'basic unit' of the Church. Protestants place a great stress upon the role of the Holy Spirit in the life of the believer. It is he who convicts an individual and leads them to faith by illuminating the message of the gospel. The Church is deprived of any direct role in ministering salvation. Salvation becomes a direct and immediate action between God and the believer. This is the basis of the Reformation slogans such as *sola gratia* (grace alone) and *sola scriptura* (Scripture alone). These slogans do not negate the importance of Church and ministry; rather they emphasise the directness of the individual's experience of God. The 'alone' of the slogans could thus be seen as directed primarily against the mediating role of the Church. This Protestant principle of *immediacy* leads to an emphasis upon the personal appropriation of faith and conversion, personal prayer and Bible study. The centre of spirituality becomes personal prayer and Bible reading.

Catholics, however, begin with the community. For Catholics, the community is the 'basic unit' of the Church.[19] Spirituality is not a private affair. This is based on the Catholic principle of *communion*. *Communion* refers to the Catholic belief that no one comes alone to God. In Acts 2, the Holy Spirit descended upon individuals as a group or community. This is not to say that the relationship is not *personal*, but it is to stress that it is not *private*. We often equate 'personal' with 'private', but the two are not synonymous. The centre of spirituality here becomes the communal celebration; that is, the Eucharist or Holy Communion. Of course, personal prayer is still important but even here its traditional forms tend to be community-orientated, such as the Liturgy of Hours (often called 'the Prayer of the Church'). It is obligatory for all bishops, priests and deacons to pray this each day, and it is also recommended that laity do the same.

In Catholicism, the principle of communion has implications which many Protestants find difficult. Catholics have no difficulty in using family terms within the community. The priest is called 'Father', the nun is called 'Sister', and the Bishop of Rome is called 'Pope', '*il Papa*'. Because community is basic, there is also no difficulty including those members who have died within the community. Death does not break communion in Christ and so does not separate those in the 'Church in heaven' from those in the 'Church on earth'. Similarly, Catholics have no problem with Mary, the Mother of Jesus, simply because no family (community) has any problem with 'Mother'.

The principle of communion also explains the Catholic Church's belief that she plays a mediating role in the economy of salvation. Again we must stress that this does not detract from what is said in Scripture:

> For there is one God; there is also one mediator between God and humankind, Christ Jesus, himself human, who gave himself a ransom for all (1 Tim. 2:5, NRSV).

Rather, this mediating role is understood to relate to how

people even know about the gospel. Since the gospel's truth is unavailable to unaided human reason, it must be told or revealed. This revelation was made by God in Jesus. The responsibility of relating this to today's world is entrusted to the Church (2 Cor. 5:18). Thus the Church acts as a 'mediator' between the gospel and the people of this world.

> The one mediator, Christ, established and ever sustains here on earth his holy Church, the community of faith, hope and charity, as a visible organisation through which He communicates truth and grace to all men.[20]

These principles clearly have profound ecclesiological implications, but in terms of spirituality the two are not incompatible. Stressing the immediacy and intimacy of relationship between God and humans does not necessarily negate the importance of community, and vice versa. The two should not be separated. The community cannot become a substitute for personal spirituality. Similarly, personal spirituality should not become more important than the communal sharing of faith. A community of faith should consist of individuals of faith. Our faith does have to be 'grasped', as the Reformers put it, but it is not to be held exclusively for ourselves (Matt. 25:14–30).

Protestants can learn from Catholics the importance of community in the individual's spiritual life. In the body there is great strength. It is interesting to go through the letters of St Paul and see how often he addresses not individuals but communities. Indeed many Scripture passages are read in a personal way when in fact they are addressed to communities and only make sense when understood in that way.

The Church is emphatically not an agglomeration of pious individuals who happen to believe the same gospel. Yet all too often Christians talk about 'my Christian life, my faith, my salvation, my relationship with God'.

Passages about the work and gifts of the Holy Spirit, about spiritual warfare, about guidance or prayer, are often applied in an individualistic way. The letters of Paul and Peter are often expounded as though addressed to individual Christians, whereas the vast majority of them were written to churches.[21]

Personal faith comes from community and leads to community. On a practical level, it is interesting to note how many Protestant churches, with their insistence upon the faith of the individual, are nevertheless vibrant *fellowships*. Meanwhile many Catholic parishes, with their stress upon community, sometimes seem to lack the vibrancy of Christian community. This is a great irony. It is here that Catholics can learn from Protestants. Individuals of faith will reach out to others. Believing individuals will form community. But individuals need to be evangelised. Often the word 'community' is replaced by 'fellowship' among Protestants. This is telling. A fellowship is a group of individuals together *as individuals*. A community is a group of individuals who are together in *belonging*. While community remains at the level of fellowship, division will be possible. When individuals, *as individuals*, disagree it is easy to divide. If these individuals *belong* to one another, division is far less likely. This is the strength of the Catholic view of *community* and, by extension, of the Catholic Church.

Community and Evangelism

Our modern Western world is such that issues of community and individuality are important. Politicians speak of the need for community while more and more people are isolated and lonely. There is the desire for community but the experience of alienation. It is a common event to travel to another, quite different, culture and experience what we call 'culture shock'. Our own culture, however, is invisible to us. It is like the back of our head – we know it is there but never see it.

Modern Western culture is often described as 'post-Enlightenment'.[22] The Enlightenment began in the eighteenth century. This was when humans were said to have 'come of age'. In many ways it was a cultural 'conversion experience'. Fundamental to this experience was the belief that science held the key to all of nature. Isaac Newton showed how previously mysterious forces could be explained with simple mathematics. Nature could now be explained without reference to purpose or causes. Miracles, divine intervention and providence had no place and, should God be conceived of, he tended to be the distant onlooker of eighteenth-century deism. It was the Age of Reason. Immanuel Kant threw down the challenge to all, 'Dare to know!' This challenge was addressed to the rational individual, who was autonomous and independent, with inherent rights and potential. The independent nation states arose and progress was the order of the day. This progress, however, was no longer seen in terms of divine purpose or will but as the fulfilment of the potential of human reason, unfettered by dogma and superstition.

The common cry that science has 'disproved' religion is an obvious one. The laws of economics began to be better understood and managed. If gravity and the motion of the planets could be understood by rules and laws, so could commerce and industry. Individuals became useful rather than valuable. They became units in the process of production. As the Industrial Revolution drew people away from their family homes, the extended family was shattered,[23] cities grew and families shrank. There was also a partition set up between the world of 'facts' or 'laws' and the world of 'opinions' or 'beliefs'. Facts could be proved, beliefs were unprovable and therefore only conjecture. Matters of belief and religion were seen as internal and private.

This is an ill-defined, hasty outline, yet the Enlightenment did bring benefits. Human rights were recognised and prosperity established. But other consequences were less predictable and less beneficial. The hope of progress – the dream of the establishment of the kingdom on earth by human development – was shattered by the horrors seen in the trenches of the Somme in the First World War. Economics was shown to be fallible as the stockbrokers jumped to their deaths on Wall Street in 1929. Disillusion, confusion and alienation became the order of the day. And now even the alternatives such as Marxism seem to be tarnished.

The fact that the present time is termed 'post-Enlightenment' suggests that something new is afoot. Around us we see the signs of decay as our culture crumbles and yet we do not know what is replacing it. There is a profound alienation in our culture. Our society is no longer monochrome and predictable. Rather, it is dazzling in its variety and cosmopolitan array. There is an unpredictability and uncertainty which is common. As far back as the sixties, people were heralding the no-future generation. Perhaps now we have arrived at the no-concern generation. In a world of insecurity, the individual's identity is shaky. If I can trust nothing, with what can I identify? There is thus a turning inward and a spiritual hunger in our world today. Part of this hunger is for purpose. The Enlightenment sought to explain the world without recourse to talk of 'purpose'. Now the Enlightenment has faded, people are once again seeking purpose. For some this is found in the New Age or oriental mystical religions, for others in atheistic materialism. We must offer Christ, and a realistic, healthy, practical and lived prophetic community.

We have seen that our society is fragmented and the value of individuals barely recognised. We have seen that the local community and the community of the family are shattering. We must see that people need to be acknowledged as individuals of worth who are accepted in community. Thus, both the stress on the individual and the importance of community are essential for the effective evangelisation of our culture. In 1992, a major survey of how people come to Christian faith was published.[24] The most important factor which was noted in becoming Christian was personal contact with other Christians, whether spouses or friends.[25] Thus people became interested when approached and accepted as individuals. However, conversion was not usually sudden. A process was commonly involved, as the inquirer attended Christian meetings and became integrated into a body of believers.[26] Our world is inhabited by individuals, many of whom recognise a need for belonging. An understanding of the insights of both Catholic and Protestant approaches can meet the needs of our times.

The Catholic Church must recognise that individuals need

to express their individuality within the community and have the opportunity to play their part. In many Catholic parishes this possibility is sometimes restricted. The Catholic Church has to implement its belief in the ministry of the laity.

> A new state of affairs today both in the Church and in social, economic, political and cultural life, calls with a particular urgency for the action of the lay faithful. If lack of commitment is always unacceptable, the present time renders it more so. It is not permissible for anyone to remain idle.[27]

Many Protestant churches seem to attract the young and skilled, who are recognised and used. This may be because Protestantism is attractive to those of a particular social standing, individuals who are benefiting from the exercise of their individuality.[28] Whatever the case, the individual cannot be allowed to get lost in the crowd. The individual needs community but also needs individual purpose.

Our evangelism of this culture needs to hold in balance the individual and community dimensions of the gospel. The Protestant emphasis on the individual and the Catholic emphasis on the community are both important.[29] We must call for individual conversion but also the conversion of structures and society. Today the individuals to be evangelised are found both inside our churches and outside. Inside our churches are those on the pilgrimage of conversion and outside are those whom we must call to join us. We must recognise individuals with their needs but also the needs of community. This will always be the unresolved tension.

8

Community – Yearning of a Secular Society

If one word had to be found to describe our present secular society in the West perhaps none would have a better claim to prominence than 'uncertainty'. This uncertainty may not always be explicitly articulated but underlying much of our culture runs a deep seam of insecurity. Perhaps the sheer volume and speed of change which our society has experienced has had an important influence in this respect. In a world of idolised progress, how can certainties be clung to? People need security to rear families, to build careers, to feel that their present efforts have some sense and meaning, usually in terms of future benefit. However, Jürgen Moltmann has suggested that over our present Western society there hangs a banner proclaiming, 'No future'.[1] This, he seems to imply, comes from a disillusionment with the promised 'brave new world' which progress was supposed to bring, a disillusionment which has bred hopelessness and restlessness. As the future is insecure and the present full of restless uncertainty, people turn to the past. Our society often seems to yearn for the golden age of yesteryear when certainties ruled and security could be found around the hearth or the family meal table. Our society seems to yearn for true community.

What are the defining features or moods we can identify with regard to community? It is first worth noting that our society seems to be undergoing a period of transition. This means that generalisations are difficult to safely make. There are many paradoxes, tensions and contrary streams to our society. One part of the culture may present one set of values while another may champion attitudes of a quite different nature. The oppositions which exist are often radical and, sometimes, violent. There is an incredible diversity abroad.

> The origins and/or causes of the profound changes in the 'wholeness' of cultures have been attributed to any number of different factors. On a more specific level, a diverse group of literary and social historians have begun a thorough re-examination of the changing nature of . . . [culture].[2]

This overarching variety is often referred to as 'post-modernism'. Modernism symbolised the uniting of all things under a commonly held reason to which all had access. Progress could then be made which would free humanity from the bondage of superstition and ignorance into the brightness of enlightenment. Post-modernism signifies the breakdown and imminent collapse of this optimistic world-view. However, even post-modernism is subject to a range of definitions. Whatever the case, it seems that diversity and its attendant tensions are thriving in our present culture. One of these tensions which we can identify has been present virtually throughout the history of society. This is the tension between the 'one' and the 'many'.

The One and the Many

The tension which exists between the 'one' and the 'many' can be seen as a pendulum which swings between unity and diversity. At some times or in some places the pendulum will swing towards the 'one', that is, towards unity. In this case, commonality is treasured. All people are seen as essentially similar. Unity is therefore seen as possible and desirable. Sometimes this means that the individuals within a society are lost within the identity of the group. It is the group, the tribe, the family or the nation which is primary.

On the other hand, at different times or places the dialectical pendulum will swing towards the 'many'. When this happens, diversity is held to be of paramount importance. Individual expression and variety is treasured, often in contradistinction to the group or society. With such diversity, tolerance and absolute freedom are desirable. Here society is seen as simply a collection of essentially separate individuals. Margaret Thatcher famously summed up this approach when she boldly declared, 'There is no such thing as society.' True community lies somewhere between unity and diversity, in that rare place where individuals find a home within the group but are nevertheless respected and treasured as individuals and not just as cogs or components within a greater and more important wheel.

This tension has its roots almost as far back in philosophy as we can go. Heraclitus (*c*. 536–*c*. 470 BC) felt that the world was basically a place of chaos, where there is a constant flux leading to diversity and movement, all things tending to fragmentation and diversification. The basic fact of the natural world is thus strife and the basic state of humanity is conflict. Parmenides (born *c*. 515 BC), pictured a totally unchanging unity underlying all things, despite their variety, and tending to harmony. For Heraclitus, then, the 'many' always precedes the 'one', while Parmenides 'is the philosopher of the One *par excellence*'.[3] Since their day society has swung between a preference for the one and for the many.

Modernism: The One

Present Western society has its proximate roots in the revolution of thought and attitude which Europe underwent in the Enlightenment of the seventeenth century. The thinkers of this time self-consciously sought to establish a universal order based solely upon reason. Reason was a capacity to which, in theory at least, all people had common access. Such reason transcended cultural expression and variety. If reason could be embraced and utilised then everyone would abide by its self-evident tenets and live accordingly in harmony. This would lead to progress and peace, since all would agree through reasonable debate based upon commonly held and accessible truths.

> Sustained by a steadfast faith in absolute values and the universality of objective principles, this classical age has been one of comparative cultural stability. Even when a thinker like Descartes questioned the validity of traditional philosophy, he still retained confidence in the power of reason ... and the possibility of reaching absolute certainty.[4]

One of the aims of this time was to free people from the tutelage of superstition and unreasonable belief. There was thus a strong individualistic element involved. The individual was essentially more important than the community. Some would point to this process beginning even before the Enlightenment. Burckhardt, for instance, has pointed to the Renaissance of the fourteenth century as the time when the fundamental shift in self-understanding took place.[5] This shift involved the person seeing himself for the first time as essentially and primarily an individual. However, Burckhardt's theory fails to account for the strong communal aspects of the Renaissance and late mediaeval society. Nevertheless, there may be some truth in the assertion that the individual emerged from the crowd in the late mediaeval period. The Reformation, for instance, was perhaps in part based upon this priority which was accorded to the individual; thence the Reformers' insistence upon the faith of the individual over the received practice of the Church (community).

Despite the high place given to individuals by the Enlightenment, there was an overshadowing importance accorded to universals (the 'one'). Reason was the basis of truth. Collectivism overshadowed individuality. This is clear when we examine Enlightenment-inspired movements. The United States was perhaps *the* Enlightenment nation. An interesting sign of the implicit collectivism of modernity is still shown on US coins. There one still finds the legend '*E Pluribus Unum*', that is, 'One out of many'. In a more extreme form, the same collectivism was seen in the earliest days of the Enlightenment as the totalitarianism of the French Revolution extinguished dissent and all divergent individual expression was violently quashed.

Similarly, in the present century, the ground has been fertile for collectivist doctrines of all shades, from communism to the national socialism of Nazi Germany. The modern period has proved more amenable to such large-scale collectivist tendencies than any other era. Indeed, modernism, despite its variety, has shown a marked tendency to totalitarianism, albeit often in the supposedly benign and usually subtle form of 'Westernisation' and 'secularisation'.

Post-modernism: The Many

Post-modernism is not a united movement or approach. Its common feature is ironically its diversity. Although it is often said that our period is 'post-modern' this is something of an oversimplification. We live in an age where modernism still holds sway alongside decidedly post-modern influences. This is one of the sources of tension, uncertainty and insecurity in our culture. On the 'modernist' side, the world continues apace towards ever greater degrees of unity, instanced in such ventures as the supranational trading blocs taking shape across the world. At the same time, on the 'post-modernist' side, there is a growing nationalism of a virulence and fervour which is increasingly dividing the world, from the outright warfare of the Balkans to the more democratic nationalist movements in Scotland, Wales, Northern Italy, Quebec, Australia and elsewhere. The threat of a new isolationist republicanism in the United States and Euro-sceptic conservatism in the UK show a similar move away from wider unity.

In terms of community, this creeping diversity in our culture shows itself as a rise in *individualism*. Post-modernism posits a breakdown in the communicative usefulness of language. Thus, true communication between different cultures and indeed between individuals is said to be virtually impossible. If such radical diversity is accepted then we are left with alienation and a consequent loneliness.

When the concept of the 'one' is taken to its extreme, then individuality is lost in favour of grey conformity. However, when the 'many' is taken to its own conclusion, individuality is similarly lost in absolute isolation. The path of wholeness must lie between the two, in a balance where the 'one' and the 'many' are held together in a balance. This is bound to be a difficult task, but it is the challenge of community.

Community involves *interdependence*. This, however, is often scorned in our culture. Because of its roots in the idea of the 'one' there is a certain *dependence* inculcated into members of our society. Simultaneously, because of the influence of the 'many', there is a tendency to *independence*. Both coexist in our culture. Our culture is apparently unable to move beyond a continual battle between collectivism and individualism. In the midst of this struggle, community gets overlooked.

In the UK, the struggle between the dependence related to the 'one' and the independence related to the 'many' can be seen politically. In very general terms, the Labour party could be seen as the traditional party of the 'one'. Thus, traditional Labour policies have included nationalisation and centralisation, and an emphasis on social services and union movements. The logical conclusion of this is totalitarianism. On the other hand, the Conservative party has been seen to occupy the other extreme. The Conservatives are the party of the 'many' where individual freedom is all-important. Therefore, traditional Conservative policies have been a decrease in bureaucratic involvement in people's affairs, a free market, the personal provision of social care, privatisation and so on. Absolute freedom is seen as an absolute right, the logical conclusion of which is not freedom (which always involves some restriction) but anarchy. One tends towards dependence

(Labour) and the other to independence (Conservative). Both, however, miss the path of community because both are by-products of modernism.

Increasingly, there is a feeling of disillusionment with traditional politics. So in the 1992 UK General Election, the Natural Law Party, espousing New Age solutions such as meditation and 'yogic flying', were able to field candidates in every contested seat. Despite their failure to actually gain any of these seats, their sheer presence on the political scene says something about the disillusionment that exists. The need is for community and true community involves interdependence.

Church – Culture – Community

Does the Church have anything specific to say to the world as regards community? If she is true to her nature, she has a great deal to say. First though, we must briefly look at the role the Church has played in creating the type of secular society we see around us because the Church is not immune from blame for the present malaise. The relationship between Church and culture has, throughout history, been reciprocal. The failure of the Christian Church to present a credible and united voice to the world has led in directly to our present situation.

The Catholic and Protestant Churches have often been seen as at opposite extremes. The Catholic Church has been castigated as a monolithic Roman beast devouring all in its path, while Protestants have been dismissed as anarchic and disunited individualists split by chaotic infighting. The antagonism of the Catholic–Protestant debate became polarised into a battle between the 'one' and the 'many'. In the immediate post-Reformation era, neither experienced the real embrace of community where the 'one' and the 'many' are held in a delicate but sacred balance. Even now, in these days of ecumenism, the witness to community is still maimed by the damage done to the body of Christ. Present Western secular society evolved in the shadow of the Church's dislocation.

It was the contention of Max Weber in 1930[6] that Western capitalism and the Calvinistic Reformed tradition were intimately linked. It is from his thesis that we get the term 'Protestant work ethic'. It must be clearly stated that it was not Weber's thesis that capitalism was *caused* by Calvinism. For him, capitalism existed long before the Reformation dawned. However, he did identify a new 'spirit of capitalism' which emerged in the early modern period. It was this modern capitalism which he linked with the emergence of Protestantism. The reasons he posited for this included Protestantism's assurance that an individual could find salvation within the world and not just by withdrawal from it.[7] As McGrath states, 'a connection between Calvin's world-affirming theology and capitalism seems inevitable.[8] Capitalism is very much the politic of the 'many', and it would seem that we can find Christian roots to this approach.

Similarly, Christian roots can be found for the politics of the 'one'. We need only recall the number of times Marxism has been called a Christian heresy. In a way, it was an attempt to have the kingdom without the king.[9] Because Marxism is a politics of the 'one', just as capitalism is of the 'many', it is not surprising that for the best part of a century the two stood looking askance at one another over a crevasse of fear. Brave pioneers like Vaclav Havel in the Czech Republic have sought a middle way,[10] but in general the two have remained unreconciled, despite the fall of the Berlin wall and the opening of the East in 1989. Thus the failure of Christianity to maintain the integrity of its witness has spawned both collectivist tyranny and individualist dehumanisation and the two still present themselves as the sole options to our world of need. The Church must show the middle way clearly. This is a real possibility as long as ecumenical dialogue continues, embracing the Protestant emphasis on the individual and the Catholic emphasis on the community.

To show how the 'one' and the 'many' can be reconciled, we must turn to the Trinity. It took the Church virtually five centuries to unfold and begin to understand the Trinity. Central to this process were the so-called Cappadocian fathers of the later fourth century: St Basil the Great, St Gregory of Nazianzus and St Gregory of Nyssa. Debate had centred around how the one God and Father of biblical revelation could be reconciled with the divinity of the Son, Jesus, and the Holy Spirit. It would seem that God was *both* 'one' and 'many', two poles which were essentially irreconcilable as far as philosophy was concerned. The Cappadocians, however, did reconcile the two in a way which would enter orthodox Christian teaching as the most adequate of the Trinitarian paradox. God, the proposed, could be seen as having one substance but three persons. In the thought of the Cappadocians, the 'one' and the 'many' were thus reconciled. In God is to be found both 'one' and 'many', one and three in 'tri-unity', or Trinity.

Where Plato had pointed to commonality as pre-eminent over individuality and Aristotle had pointed to the individuals from whom commonality emerged, the Cappadocians pointed to the Trinity, where individuality and commonality existed eternally. There was thus no necessary tension between 'one' and 'many' nor between commonality and individuality. In the Trinity, the Church finds her source and model. In his letter to the Ephesians, St Paul writes, 'I bow my knees before the Father [*Pater*], from whom every family [*patria*] in heaven and on earth takes its name' (Eph. 3:14–15 NRSV). Assuming Paul was not merely making a clever Greek pun it would seem that communities here on earth are somehow seen to reflect that of God himself. This has enormous implications for the Christian approach to community and its witness of community in a world where community is debased and individuality exalted. Christian community is to reflect the community of the Trinity.

The Christian Witness of Community

The basic unspoken message of the world is that the individual and the community are in opposition. The real individual is the one who cannot find expression within the narrow restrictions of community. The two are thus placed in opposition. One possible solution would be the extremes of individualism or collectivism we have been examining. Either the individual is given complete free reign or the collective is given complete prominence.

The Christian approach is very different. The Christian must acknowledge the tension which exists between individual and community but this tension does not necessarily imply an opposition. Christianity often deals in paradox as it tackles matters beyond the scope of human knowledge. In the area of community we face paradox. In the Christian schema, the individual should be realised in the context of community. Community only makes sense as individuals freely enter into and choose it. The two co-exist and are inseparable. This reflects the eternal coincidence of 'one' and 'many' within the Godhead itself.

Colin Gunton explains the relationships within the Trinity thus:

> The persons do not simply enter into relations with one another, but are constituted by one another in the relations. Father, Son and Spirit are eternally what they are by virtue of what they are from and to one another.[11]

The same must be said of human community. Individuals are made by community and come to full life through community. That is not to say that community is ontologically prior to individuality, since community is always constituted by individuals just as individuals are in turn constituted by community. The Fall was a symbolic breaking of communal bonds leading to alienation and the impossibility of self-fulfilment. While living in the state of the Fall, it is impossible for humans to be what they are made to be; that is, beings in communion.[12] Communion constitutes the fullness of life. This is the essential message the Church has to bring to the world. This present secular world searches for being, without communion, in terms of individually realised self-fulfilment. Rather, it seeks communion in such things as transient sexual experience. The Church proclaims that community and being are inseparable. The community to which the Church must point is primarily the community at the heart of God's triune life. As Christians we are 'in Christ' and this must imply that we have been assumed into the very life of the Trinity itself. Christian community here on earth is only an outworking of the true reality of community amongst redeemed humanity hidden for us in Christ's Trinitarian life in heaven.

Church – Cult – Community

Our task as Sion Community involves working with young people in schools and in parishes. Because we are known as a community, the young people sometimes come to us and ask us, are we a cult? However, the difference between us as a community and a cult is vast; yet because cults are prominent at the moment in a few of the 'soaps', the assumption is made by some people that a healthy, authentic community can be mistaken for a cult.

Many television programmes, books and articles about religious cults begin with stories of painful or embarrassing incidents that first brought to their authors' attention the fact that young people had begun to experiment with novel and often frightening forms of religious community. The impression is sometimes given that the struggles, anguish, anger and suspicion directed against cults are the most important thing about them. From the beginning, cults were pictured in the media and in books as controversial and threatening. Each group is indelibly marked as problematic, to say the least. However, it could be said that cults initially set out to fulfil an ideal, the most basic aspect of which is community. In an age when there is widespread indifference to organised religion, it is inevitable to see the growth of the cult movement.

> Modern man appears to suffer acutely from his loss of emotional reassurance . . . This anxiety-making result of the 'death' of God, so familiar in the West, has led to many attempts to fill the vacuum by a religion similar in some ways to historic Christianity but substantially new.[1]

In time, the cult movement took on more aspects than that of community. The alleged greed and unscrupulousness of the founders and leaders of cults were highlighted by those who wished to expose their alleged manipulativeness. There were scares and scandals about allegations of some cults buying influence in political circles. In the period following the deaths at Waco in the United States (1993) and in Japan (1994), people became more aware of the destructive influence of cults. Since then there have been legal battles involving a small number of cults. In conjunction with contemporary concerns about the legality of the practice of some religious groups, the controversy has spilled over into debates as to whether the Church is meeting deep emotional needs. The terms that are used of cults are controversial. The complications lie in the fact that the sociologists and Church theologians disagree over the most appropriate terminology to define 'cult'. 'Cult' has a fashionable and respectable note among some sociologists:

> The tendency for sects to become denominations has frequently been noted and on the basis of this tendency the generalisation has sometimes been made that a sect-type organisation can exist for only a generation, that

in the second generation the sect becomes a church or a denomination.[2]

The important point to establish here is that I use 'cult' in its popular sense to refer to groups, considered small, inward-looking, unorthodox, weird and possibly threatening. I hope that this is a widespread public view of cults.

From Church to Cults

No one would deny that this century has seen the greatest growth in the ecumenical movement for the reunion of the divided Christian Churches; yet it has also seen the fastest expansion of new Christian sects and cults. The reality of our time is that the great move towards *unity* is counterbalanced by a new emergence of split, heresy and schism. Some cults can no longer be regarded as harmless deviations from the historic norms of the Christian faith, liturgy and behaviour. Some have demonstrated a remarkable growth in numbers, using modern means of propaganda. These sects disseminate their views by using enthusiastic missionaries as well as the printed page and other media. If their work was only among 'pagans' or the uncommitted of the modern world, then concern for their success might be limited, yet in some cases they target practising Christians and seduce them away from their Church.

The high-priestly prayer of Christ in John 17 is that 'they all may be one'. It is clear from this prayer that Jesus wished his believing community to manifest on earth the divine love he has with the Father. The root objection I have to sects and cults is that they provide for a world already divided into political, racial and social camps, which leads not to unity but rather to arrogance, competition and split. Thus the death of Christ, which is about reconciliation, is betrayed by a Christian Church not at one with itself. The churches themselves have been at fault and the new sects and cults have splintered the Church even further. The bewilderment and confusion caused by cults is strikingly illustrated in their competitiveness and arrogance which is usually centred on a charismatic figure.

> A cult has a living leader. He is not elected by man but is supposedly appointed by God, unless he happens conveniently to be God. He cannot be ejected or replaced by the members and if he dies the cult falls apart unless someone else sets himself up on the vacated throne.[3]

This leader usually has a 'new', questionable truth for society. It is undeniable that many sects and cults come into being because the existing churches or denominations have lost their zeal and fervour. They become strongholds of the safe and comfortable, and often the habitat of the respectable middle classes. New cults show all the characteristics of being the church of the disinherited. As their members rise economically and culturally, then the first fervour is compromised and the world-renouncing ethics for which the cult stands is rescinded. Suspicious of an educated ministry or formal liturgy and ceremonials, these cults and sects find the greatest satisfaction in the emotional freedom and naive supernaturalism, the vivid personal sermons with rhetorical devices and the forms of church government which the parent church has outgrown. Honesty, thrift, abstinence, penance, simplicity of lifestyle and diligence reflect their economic position. It is also very significant that in almost all of these groups millennialism has spread. All of the above are the defence mechanisms of the disinherited. The leaders of these cults love the God who will 'put down the mighty' and vindicate their faith because it promotes greater community and the elimination of the social tensions.

Cultism has also its own distinctive code of ethics; often settling around the whims of its leader, even sometimes for their sexual gratification. This was true of the leader of the Waco cult. Their standards of ethics are usually legalistic, rigid and puritanical, with a black and white morality which divides men and women all too easily, not to mention the children who often are kept separate from their parents. Following hard on the heels of these ethical standards will emerge condemnation of any practice of the opulent. Worldly amusement, dancing, cinema and the use of tobacco and alcohol are frequently banned.

There is a strange attractiveness about this simplistic, world-renouncing ethic of the cult and it usually provides their communities with firm cohesive and unifying dogmas. Nevertheless, this is a naive simplicity because the world cannot be divided so conveniently into sinners and saints because both cohabit in the same person. Cultism has its gigantic temptation to arrogance, pride and uncharitableness. Condescension is the hallmark of its being. It has a self-righteousness that can condemn others while subtly elevating itself into a position of worthiness which goes far beyond its actual members.

It can happen that the members of local churches make people feel unwelcome. This then cuts off the lifeline to some and can produce emotional starvation. Emotions today are highlighted and therefore if people feel unwelcome in churches they can be driven into the arms of the cults.

> Interpersonal bonds are now widely viewed as providing fundamental support for recruitment . . . There is a high level of affective arousal and the affective content is primarily positive – loving.[4]

A considerable number of churchgoing people find their social and emotional life outside the churches, despite a deep longing and desire to do so within the context of the Church. The cults on the whole provide for the whole of people's lives. Indeed, the cults devise means to stir up emotions, and with complete sincerity attribute the results to the direct activity of God. That can be taken a stage further. Sects can insist that an emotional reaction is the only proof that the individual person has made direct contact with God. Christianity or another religion for them, then, becomes a religion of feelings. Their meetings therefore become highly charged with emotions and a simplistic liturgy. Preaching can become passionate denunciation of the worldly, horrific accounts of hell. The appeal is rarely to reason but almost always to the emotions.

Another characteristic of cults is their craving for certainty and authority. One of their great cries is that the mainline church leaders do not speak out on issues of great importance. Maybe the Churches fail people in their silence on major and sensitive issues. There is a fear that leadership can isolate people by coming out strongly; yet people need clear guidance. The cults give them strong guidance and also clear parameters of authority. The members of the cults demand certainty of their leaders, since they have enough doubt of their own. Strong authority and a black and white code of ethics give them respite from the responsibility of weighing motives, intentions and results. Cults are usually suspicious of tradition and are at pains to point out that somewhere the Christian Church went wrong and they in turn have been sent by God to turn it from apostasy. Because of their overemphasis on authority, licence is then given for leadership to emerge in a form little short of dictatorship. Allied to this is the assurance that their little group is the only one which is right.

Some cults work on racial and social minorities which have slipped through the Church's net. These cults do their recruiting in the areas of drug addiction, social deprivation, alcoholism and even ethnic minorities. Here the Church is weak in its outreach. Perhaps the greatest area of failure on the part of the established Churches is with young people. We have not been culturally relevant, and yet when these cults evangelise our youth under our noses we are powerless or unwilling to do anything about it. We have driven some Black people into cult movements because of sectarianism. This has led the Black cult leader, Mrs Ethel Christian, to claim that she could prove from Scripture that Jesus was a Negro.[5] If local churches, by racial or class prejudices, have become enclaves of complacency and individualism, then we Christians must bear the blame for the alienation which has resulted in more sects and cults setting themselves up as communities. If the modern Church has diluted its beliefs with compromise then we are to blame for the search which is fulfilled in cults.

At present in the Church there is too much isolation and individualism which is a ripe breeding ground for the new sects and cults.

The proliferation of utopian communal groups, arising out of the 1960s raises once again the question of the role religion might play in the creation and survival of such groups. A common view... is that society at large is becoming progressively more secular.[6]

However, the Church is always in need of reformation. The challenge of the cults is a summons to reformation. If the gospel of the Church is set forth as a community of supernatural clarity which condemns the respectability of this world, then the zeal and fanaticism of cultic aggressiveness can be curbed. The essence of Christian communication must be love in community which sets hearts afire and fulfils human needs. The Church must, in the final analysis, not only outwit and outthink the cultic revolution but must 'out-live' it.

Cults and Community Living
Human beings are social. Our families form our first social group. The family into which we are born has enormous influence upon us, not only because the long and complex learning process takes place before adulthood and self-sufficiency are attained, but also because the family becomes the example for all social groups. Conformity to characteristic views, dress and conduct differentiate social groupings, marking the most rebellious as well as the most conventional. Imitation of our peers is basic to learning and development and the family group is an important influence throughout our lives.

The tendency to see an action as more appropriate

when others are doing it works well normally. As a rule, we will make fewer mistakes by acting in accord with social evidence than contrary to it. Usually when a lot of people are doing something, it is the right thing to do.[7]

But every society provides numerous examples of group influence which turned out to be injurious to the group itself as well as being harmful to others. Freud believed that the influence of a group could be traced back to the primitive horde.[8] Just as primitive mankind survives potentially in every individual, so the primal horde arises out of any random collection of people. We Christians disagree with this statement of Freud and answer by offering the suggestions that man and woman seek community because this is the way God intended us to live. Certainly whatever theoretical model one might prefer, the desire for community living and approval remains with us as a very powerful controlling force.

Numerous experiments show how a group can change the perceptions of its members. A group can even foster and maintain a bizarre, paranoid view of things. People can feel secure in a group but its protection has its price. Compliance with the group often extends further than just accepting the group's views. Disapproval, punishment or rejection can occur when a member voices criticism of the consensus or disagrees with the leader. The dissident is shown to be disloyal, lacking commitment or obstructing the important work of the group. Pressures like these are present in all groups but they are intensified in a cult. Sometimes extreme dependence on the cult community is fostered by isolating the member from other sources of stimuli such as wife, husband, parents or children. This cuts off emotional closeness to family and consequently the cult's ability to reward or punish is enhanced. It is not surprising, then, that in extreme cults an attack on couples and family life is enforced.

> The intrusive role of a brainwashing scenario is driving a moral wedge between the close relations of members and . . . the Unification Church [Moonies].[9]

Such separation of families smacks of manipulation. The attack on marriage and family life within cults is widespread. Pressure towards group sex or sexual relationships with the leader is substituted to cement the bonding needed to hold the cult together. Some even have degenerated as far as 'free love'.

> Every member had sexual access to every other with his or her consent, while fidelity was negatively sanctioned; preference of one member for another was quickly discouraged. When two members of the community showed a marked preference of one member for one another, they were asked to mate with two others.[10]

The major way that cults control their members is through the threat of censure and expulsion. Moral principles are often violated to further the cult's success. The leader can justify immoral actions as being necessary for the greater good of the cult. When this happens, the importance of each individual and their dignity is lowered. The cult is usually seen as having a divine mission and it is in this context that a liberalism is given to leadership to pursue its own ends. Compliance in this way increases the members' psychological dependence upon the group. To leave the group would mean that all sacrifices had been in vain. It can also highlight the cult as more valuable than it is. The withholding of important information is another attribute of power within the cult. Things are put under the carpet, even cruelty and unethical living. Compliance to the group becomes the norm.

Cults: Why Do They Flourish?

The first question asked by people about cults is, 'Why do cults experience such a high degree of apparent success in their recruitment?' After all, the Western world is a rational place. We in the First World pride ourselves in being fulfilled and happy in our materialism and technology. Yet we are losing the significance of the individual as we focus our attention more and more on generalities. We are saturated with reports that proclaim new troubling problems, each of which suggests its own doomsday effect. Military and political conflict, pollution, inflation and conservation of energy have joined nuclear weapons as signposts that lead to our cultural Armageddon.[11]

We all know people who are increasingly lonely, although some of these people do not live alone. As I ride on buses, on trains and planes, I gaze into empty eyes. These empty eyes seem to grow more uncertain each year. The materialistic impulses of our society have given rise to a loneliness as a result of unemployment, early retirement and less working time. People need to be wanted and belong. The young can now manufacture for themselves drugs which enable them to escape whenever they don't like the way the world looks. Our culture seems to be moving from an age of medications into an age of meditation. Western people are turning towards spiritual experiences. The range of religious appeal is so wide, with some legitimate and some fraudulent claimants. The results of these appeals can be laden with disaster. Human potential movements, religious experiences, and even the drug culture produce an entire segment of society that is totally egocentric. 'What is in this for me?' is the prevailing question.

Many people today are weary of constant change. Change has become the chronic illness for millions. These people seek stability, security and simplicity. Some people, however, resist change because they do not wish to face the challenge. What could be more ideal than to enter a cult where you don't have to think or plan? Many of the cults have grown up to meet the needs of people who feel the unbearable pressure of their lifestyles. A new generation of young people is growing up in the midst of violence, assassinations, corruption in Churches, government and leadership, and several other disillusioning stresses which throw them into the arms of waiting cults.

> Zealous religions, quasi religions, and political groups are cunningly formed to achieve practical goals. Some address the disparity between members' distress and their desire for contentment by spiritual means. Others may provide relief from an addictive illness poorly managed by the medical community. Still others alleviate the intolerable consequences of perceived social oppression.[12]

People in Europe today are very mobile. We are continually

162

being uprooted, which puts a harsh strain on family life, particularly the children. They lose the opportunity to develop relationships and are continually thrown into new systems. Cult members seek simple human relationships. One cult member told me that the cult cared for him and gave him a sense of identity. Even though the outward appearance of the cult wasn't right for him, he nevertheless 'feels' that he is an important part of the group. This group offered a sense of identity and friendship which he gladly accepted.

The divorce rate is escalating, to say nothing of the fact that fewer people are getting married.[13] Some attribute the increase in divorce to a shift in moral standards; others contend that economic pressures have contributed to the failure of many marriages. Even our leisure society has contributed to family stress. How many families gather round the table for a daily common meal and communicate as they eat? Usually eating is done in isolation or in front of the television. Do we suggest time for family activity and togetherness or is sport, to mention but one alternative, so important? The number of families who consciously make an effort to bind their members together in a common lifestyle shrinks as we do 'our own thing'. This adds to deep insecurity about family ties. Cults by their nature are based around communal living. This fulfils a need in some people who feel alienated, marginalised with little or no family background.

In a family-like way, cults bind their members together, shape their attitudes and motivate them to action. These things should be the prerogative of the family, but because there is a vacuum in some people's lives in this area it is quickly pounced upon and filled by the cult. Cults have a high degree of family cohesiveness which can give them great social stability. This can even become as extreme as sharing their property. Some members join because they identify with the values of the cult because they are the values of a parent. They might believe in a philosophy of action to build an ideal world which the cult can bring about. The programmes of the cults are tailored to maximise the interest of people and 'scratch them where they itch'.

How Cults Damage Healthy Communities

The attraction to a cult lifestyle is significant in the Western world. 'Eighty-five per cent of recruits have had a religious upbringing'[14] says a television documentary. There are a variety of ways in which the cults and sects are affecting the Christian tradition in our Churches, our culture and our countries. The question is not simply about a few members of a group who are highly skilled and motivated and in total charge of their mental and emotional faculties. Other people are to be considered. What about all those people who are targeted and recruited by the group through deceptive means? What about the ordinary men and women who learn about all this 'brain-washing' from the papers and other media and are put off believing in God for life out of fear? What about all the minds that are poisoned against healthy communities? The healthy community will be looking outward to help humankind in all sorts of different ways. What do cult members have to offer the needs of the world? How can any group meet the needs of the world when it cuts itself off from the world, even from husband, wife and children relationships? In their literature, cults can state that they seek to unite the family, yet in practice families are often separated.[15]

Certainly, the teaching of the Roman Catholic Church is very clear in its task and orientation. It specifies that we are meant to be productive in the world, enhancing and encouraging growth.[16] Most cults centre on the authority of some leader who is usually a self-proclaimed teacher, visionary, prophet or 'messiah'. This self-appointed leader often claims direct revelations from God and then puts forth distinctly heretical doctrines which have their roots in the Christian Church and Scripture. The divinity of Christ is often questioned, and basic Christian morality is distorted. These groups make claim to Christianity and therefore severely damage healthy communities. Their fund-raising activities are often suspect and the money donated finds itself in the cult's financial pyramid, where the leader is top of the pyramid.

> Several ex-members admitted that [the cults'] bad image in the mass media had worried them, especially when respected outsiders had joined in the criticism.[17]

Healthy Christian communities must respond constructively rather than react with hostility to the New Age sects and cults. The victims of cults and mind control must be approached with genuine Christian love. We need to distinguish between the person who has been victimised and the power that holds them in the cult. We must be continually alert to the activities of cults so that warning can be made against the deceivers. 'Whether we are included to lead or to follow, let us hope we can see that cult behaviour is too risky, the comfort of its fantasy a lie.'[18]

Community Builders

Call to Evangelical Charismatic Christians

In 1900, Adolf Von Harnack gave a number of lectures to the students at the University of Berlin. These basically revolved around 'the essence of Christianity'. This famous Protestant theologian stressed once again the importance of the reign of God for the individual. The individual hears the good news and responds to it within. The external or the corporate is cast off. It is the individual who is redeemed and not the community. The reign of God, by extension, is no longer in the corporate; and the gospel lies beyond the realm of question because the kingdom is solely within. The words 'individual' and 'internal' occurred frequently in his talks.[1]

Von Harnack was such a learned man it must have been impossible for him to have overlooked the whole concept of community in the Scriptures and in tradition. He must have known that since its break with the Jewish community, the new Christian people have always considered themselves community (Church). Yet the extreme individualism of his theology overlooked all the valid insights of other academics and tradition. Von Harnack taught that Bible passages like the 'Sermon on the Mount' (Matt. 5:1–12; Luke 6:20–3) are mere exhortations to personal disposition and the Church is ultimately seen as a 'fellowship' of individuals, which has lost its *'Koinonia'* (community) dimension. It is merely a union of many individuals who are 'saved' through their belief in Jesus. The visible Church or community therefore is no longer important but is reduced to a 'spiritual fraternity'. It could be presumed that Von Harnack was not just on the side of those who belong to this 'invisible fellowship'. However, emphasis like this at worst invalidates, or at best simplifies the whole need for community.

One could excuse Harnack if he was the only one who propounded this individualistic understanding of Church. He is rather representative of a broad tendency among evangelical charismatics of all denominations in this century to see the reign of God at the level of the individual. Some Anglicans put it like this:

Evangelicals were concerned to respond to the evangelistic challenge . . . the participants earnestly sought ways of promoting evangelism with a 'definite emphasis on the imperative need for conversion' [personal and individual].[2]

The Free Church position could be summed up as follows: 'The essential dispositions of men are decisively altered by the Holy Spirit. Such personal transformations bring a change.'[3] The Roman Catholic charismatics would say: 'In recent times however, the Reformers' ringing affirmation of justification by faith alone has gained a more appreciative hearing even in Roman Catholic circles.'[4]

I realise that the above may not be the official teaching of these Churches; nevertheless these are believed by wide sections of their people. The Roman Catholic position on the Church is clear in her teaching in the *Dogmatic Constitution on the Church* of Vatican II. She constantly clarifies for her people the need to build community. I have to say, however, that while the Catholic Church retains the concept of community, the interpreted and lived experience is much more individualistic than could be perceived by merely reading her teaching. Individualism has marred our Churches far more than we care to admit. It has certainly coloured our thinking when it comes to concrete action.

In evangelicalism there is a 'supermarket mentality' where people move around taking a bit of this and that. We pick up what we need usually on an emotional level and leave behind the 'costly' materials. The costly material is of course the price tag that goes hand in hand with belonging to each other at a deep level, where we become responsible for each other and where we share the pain and suffering of a broken people. This then becomes more than a nice service or a quick prayer for healing but rather an exciting journey of discovery as we walk side by side through the nitty-gritty of life with each other. We as evangelical charismatics should not take for granted the way in which the average fellowship ministers to its people, believing that we have got it all. Neither should we Catholics be too sure that the issue of community is not a problem for us since the Church has always insisted upon the idea of community.

What is needed in our day is a greater awareness of the need to build community. We need to go that step further in our commitment not just to God but to each other. This will make our lifestyle and God himself more available to others.

We would not be merely quoting the Scriptures at people or asking them whether they are born again. In an age of anxiety, we need to provide an even greater opportunity for people to discover a sense of belonging, security, self-worth, dignity and self-respect. If we search for something that will raise us above the cults or indeed the generalities of 'Church', then it will be a radical belonging to each other. The successes of all renewal movements must be judged long-term on the successes of community building.

> On the front of personal holiness, purity and faith we must fight against the world's false ideologies, distorted values, godless attitudes and unrighteous way of life . . . This implies a painful and costly mission to penetrate every segment of society with a message that will both hurt and heal . . . a message of hope that offers a convincing alternative . . . for the casualties of unjust human society.[5]

Call to the Churches

The notion of the Church being an alternative society may find confusion and even resentment among some readers. The reality of the people of God, however, is both biblical and theological. The people of God in the Scriptures are understood as an alternative society. The early New Testament communities saw themselves as contrasting with the pagan society around them. In a disturbing way, the Churches in Western culture have been assimilated into political structures and governments.

> The public role of religion will not be decided by a few defeats or victories in specific elections or policy

disputes. It will be decided in large part by the capacity of various religious leaderships to liberate themselves from their captivity to political partisanships.[6]

The renunciation of violence and the search for peace is surely the greatest priority in our time. This renunciation of violence is not merely an attitude of mind but one of concrete action. Non-violence was never intended just for individuals but for nations as well. The Churches must be seen as communities who take the renunciation of violence seriously while at the same time standing in sharp contrast to secular society with its emphasis upon power and control. The exhortation of St Paul in Ephesians 5:8–9 has far-reaching consequences for the body of Christ: 'You were darkness once, but now you are light in the Lord; be like children of light, for the effects of the light are seen in complete goodness and right living and truth.' This statement clearly shows that Christians, enlightened by the Holy Spirit, are to live in accordance with the light and not with darkness. Secular society and the Church are contrasted here. The interior disposition of the converted person finds its radical consequences in the social dimension.

The so-called 'prophetic Church' of this century has on the whole been honourable and even sometimes courageous. Yet it would appear that it has been less prophetic than pacified. The Churches on the whole have been prepared to accept nature's laws and the promulgations of civil authorities more than standing vehemently in contrast to them. Particular individuals within the Churches held their ground. These single voices could be squashed with statements like 'He or she is eccentric.' However, it is not easy to silence the voice of the corporate. The crisis that the

Churches are experiencing is not 'a crisis of the Churches in the world' but rather 'a crisis of the world in the Churches'. Is it possible that the Churches have lost the power of the transcendent and therefore the world sets the agenda? We need to be a Church in the world, for the world.

For this idea to be effective, the Churches must be clear what they are offering. In a modest way, they can offer money, expertise, manpower, care and social structures. All of these things are vital but the most prophetic things they need to offer a broken world are the integration of community and the spin-offs this has in healing divisions and broken relationships. How can this challenge possibly be seen by outsiders when the Churches themselves are not united?

'I am not asking you to remove them from the world, but to protect them from the evil one. They do not belong to the world any more than I belong to the world . . . May they all be one.' This passage from John 17:15–21 surely means that when the Church lives unity then something completely new is created, something which secular society can never produce. This will inevitably become the sandpaper for the rest of society because in its reality it will show up the social and institutional deceit of ordinary structures. The structures of modern Western society are such that God (Trinity–unity) no longer figures heavily in their make-up. The moment that the Church lives the Trinitarian principle of unity, the deceit of secular structures is realised.

The Church should also be prophetic by her 'holiness'. The spiritual dimension in our society is largely in danger of being lost or distorted. The divine needs to be seen in the praying corporate body of Christ to show up the false gods of society and stop the search for spirituality being met by the New Age movement, the cults and the sects. The Churches need to live a sanctity and a sacredness that rises above the patterns of modern life. I am not advocating triumphalism or a superiority but rather a humility of alternative lifestyle that can be of service to others and not merely a condemnation of them. 'The Church's mission is neither to condemn nor to hallow but to cure.'[7]

All of this may raise many questions, but whatever way one looks at it the call to unity and the corporate dimension can never be denied. The Churches need to be deeply involved in community and deeply involved in the world.

Call to Marriage and Family Life
The sciences of anthropology, sociology and psychology tend to see the family unit as largely of cultural origin or determined by the environment or the needs of the age. History looks upon marriage and the family as being part of civilisation. Families and marriage are being affected by our rapid developing technology, mobility and mass media. For the Christian the very order of creation of man and woman, heterosexuality, biological differences and the endowment of certain masculine and feminine characteristics give us a sound base for our teaching on marriage and family relationships.

> God need not have created the world . . . He is utterly self-sufficient and His creation of life is an expression of pure love. It is in this setting of love that we must look for the formation of man, the union of the sexes in marriage and the designed ends intended to be achieved.[8]

Thus God has provided a basic order within society which can work out suitable minor details for beneficial family life. It has to be made clear that God has ordained the structure of family life in the 'covenant' relationship of marriage as the norm.

> Since the creator of all things has established the conjugal partnership as the beginning and basis of human society and by His grace has made it a great mystery in Christ and the Church (Eph. 5:32) the apostolate of married persons and of families is of unique importance for the Church and civil society.[9]

This has to be contrasted with:

> Some writers have sought to resolve these definitional [of what is a family] problems by arguing that the 'family' is what a particular social group believes it to be . . . Thus we are all engaged in defining the family.[10]

As a result of a large gap between these two positions, the family is today subject to the most unremitting scrutiny. This gives credence to the belief that an institution that was once so carefully guarded is today in jeopardy. If there is a demise of marriage and family life there will be chaos in society. So long as there is an explosion of interest in marriage and the family there is hope. Marriage is the most basic unit of community. It is the union of male and female created by the same God with dignity, rights and purpose. This equality of personhood is stressed but nevertheless men and women are different. These differences are part of God's designs and are intended to build relationships and community as well as creating community in procreation.

All of this states prophetically to the world that the family is not an accident. It is a God-centred structure based on heterosexuality. It is to be seen as the norm. Fidelity is the key to its success. The Church has always called for chastity in the marriage relationship because it is so special. Sexuality in marriage is seen as gift. The model for marriage is that of a 'covenant relationship'. This covenant relationship is seen as symbolising the covenant between God and his people. This by its very nature is unbreakable. The family unit too is designed to be unbreakable.

However, it has to be said that the family community is made up of individuals and therefore its health depends on the resources of these individuals. Personality, age, employment, unemployment and presence of children vary in all cases and therefore affect the balance of power in the family. It is God's intention that male and female complement each other. Success in the family will depend upon the power of unity. Stability is attained by many factors such as trust, fidelity, mutual respect and communication. All of these and more are necessary for the building up of this basic community. There should be a partnership so that the needs of husband, wife and children are all served. Family members are unequal in their gifts, but they are to be equal recipients of love and service.

This speaks to the world of community. While we need to be compassionate and understanding to those marriages and families that fail, we need to hold on to the sound moral code of the basic family unit. No school, no church and no other permutation can replace this small community. The family has the greatest influence in setting goals, in giving values and giving basic training. Behavioural psychologists tell us that the family is the main building-block of community.

> Marriage serves the purpose of protecting children not only through both parents, brothers and sisters and home, but also by providing them with an established system of kinship . . . [This helps] establish a proper relationship with the outside world.[11]

I do not think that we in the Christian Churches do enough to protect and encourage our married people. We preach to them on the necessity to stay together but we do not always produce the structure to hold back the 'slings and arrows' of a divorce-preoccupied culture. We need to constantly cry alarm at the easiness of divorce while at the same time welcoming those whose marriages have failed. We as Churches need to work harder at changing attitudes towards lifelong commitments and morality. We need to offer the healing ministry of Christ in a wider perspective and welcome those from broken relationships into loving communities. Marriage is a sacrament and through it family life is sacrament to society.

Call to Religious Communities

A characteristic feature of religious Orders and already established communities of all denominations over the last thirty years has been the choices by Religious of new forms of involvement within the secular world. Such involvement has frequently resulted in their joining movements for the promotion of social justice, civil rights or liberation or other worthwhile causes. There has also been a great emphasis on the growth of the individual, particularly in the area of psychology. It is not uncommon to see courses on subjects such as the Enneagram or the Myers–Briggs Personality Inventory full with Religious seeking a place in the self-actualisation dynamic of personal development. I am not suggesting that the health and wholeness of the individual within religious life is unimportant, but rather highlighting the fact that the emphasis has swung from community to individual.

The founders of religious Orders were men and women fascinated by the love of Christ and empowered by the Holy Spirit. Most of them also saw the crying need for community not just to hold their Order together but to be a challenge and an exhortation to secular society. They did not see community as just a safe haven or refuge for the weak, vulnerable or needy but rather a place of unity. This became a powerful witness.

Over the past thirty years, there has been a preoccupation with relationships among community. This can be reactionary because on the one hand there is the 'task' and on the other 'authority'. Extreme positions can be taken on board such as an overemphasis on *being* in community to the detriment of *action*, and *action* to the detriment of *being*. At the core of every founder's vision has been the desire for tough, motivated, dynamic people who were prepared to give themselves to each other and to the vision.

It is very clear that the quality of relationships in religious life is vitally important. This can be a powerful witness to the world or a display of unattractive limpness that adds to an existing overdose of apathy. Holistic community life exists for the satisfaction of its members but is closely connected with witness; in this case witness of community to an individualistic world. However, it needs to be clear that what we are witnessing to is a Trinity God and not just our spinsterhood or bachelorhood or the fear of aloneness. The common way of life for already existing communities is not something that we create from scratch, but rather one that we are called into.

Personalities differ radically, but members are held in community by the dynamic unity of God. Particular structures may change or grow but the essence of community must remain. The constant question that needs to be answered is, 'What makes the community grounded in reality?' The lifestyle of community living should revolve around love, holiness, vulnerability, sharing, mutuality, humility, forgiveness, justice, dignity and integrity. These qualities of visible community living are the *message* of the Church to the world. The central ministry of religious communities is not evangelisation, teaching, nursing, social action, fringe movements, but rather prophetic community living.

> What really is the centre of our community life? We must not shilly shally over this . . . It is really our shared life . . . which we should find in one another.[12]

The work that religious communities do must flow from who they are. It is the primary task of communities to show the world what type of God we believe in. The quality of lifestyle in some religious communities is sometimes very poor. It is so easy to hide behind the structures or share with people how good a job is being done. It is not our achievements that really matter but rather who we are as body. It is the joy and hope of community living that speaks loudly today.

The renewal of community living can differ, but essentially it revolves around prayer, sharing, forgiveness, simple lifestyle and correct ethical living. The life of prayer is essential as the launch pad for community. There are some community houses where the community members rarely meet together even to share a meal, and even more rarely to pray together. This is basically a 'motel' approach to community living. We can become so busy that we can find all sorts of excuses to avoid community prayer. We are able to share things of the mind but we also need to share our faith journey as well. If we live in community with each other then we share responsibility for each other. How many problems are allowed to flourish because of the lack of giving and receiving forgiveness? We need to question our community and personal lifestyles. There is a danger that we can take on board the consumer mentality that is all around us. What type of witness do we give to the world?

One example of this is the way we dress. For those who no longer wear clerical dress or a habit, have we replaced them with 'designer clothes'? There are instances where some Religious are so anxious to be colour co-ordinated that they have to change clothes each day. We can profess poverty but live paradoxically. The vast majority of laity do not have the money to buy new things regularly and therefore see us as enjoying a high standard of living. In this above any other age, we need to be moral in our living. The past few years have seen a number of scandals. These discredit Christian community and are a 'counter-witness'.

Even if, like every Christian, you are imperfect, you

nevertheless intend to create surroundings which are favourable to . . . each member of the community. How can this result be attained, unless you deepen in the Lord your relationships even the most ordinary ones?[13]

Let's face it, the average local church bears little resemblance to the idealism of the community which has been described in this book. Sadly, there is a movement away from community to individualism. Let us not add the names of existing religious communities to the problem, but rather let us be part of the solution. It is time for religious communities to mobilise the resource of community living and make it a productive tool for fighting against the sin of individualism.

Call to Leaders

When a society moves away from community models and towards individualism, then each person wants to be a leader. Our society is a highly organised society, yet over-organisation tends to standardise and inhibit people. Leadership, which by definition is to give direction, is inhibited today from performing its duty by individualism. Individualism has pursued individual rights and autonomy in ever new realms. This has brought confrontation between masters and servants, rich and poor, but nowhere as pronounced as between leaders and followers.

We face a profound impasse. Modern people seem to be producing a way of life that is neither individual- nor community-friendly. The average person would tend to think that their own ultimate goal is success. In the pursuit of that success, freedom is essential. Freedom is perhaps one of the most deep-seated values held by Westerners. In some ways it defines the good. It means being left alone or free from any kind of authority. However, if the whole world is made up of individuals who want to be totally free from the demands of others, then it becomes hard to forge any relationship bonds with others because such bonds will imply obligations that of essence impinge upon freedom. This is a search for a freedom from conformity to society and authority. This freedom ultimately leads to a desire to live how we want, do what we want, believe what we want, and most certainly to improve our material worlds. This makes a mockery of the most basic notions of community. This type of freedom makes community an entity which is controlled by economic opportunities and selfishness. I do not deny that there is a great desire for personal freedom and indeed the fulfilment of individual needs, yet not to the extent that the 'I' becomes the centre of the universe.

The question exists, what type of leadership is necessary to call people out of this individualism and into an attitude of community? In any study of leadership, there are as many models as there are leaders. Some have great character of person; others great abilities; others stress the relationship of leadership to structure; others set great goals and are adept at motivation. Certainly I would see the greatest need, especially in Christian circles, to be that of leadership training. A maintenance-orientated mentality that may serve institutionalism very well is acceptable as far as it goes. However, such unyielding situations as I describe above require a high calibre of talented, trained and tenacious leaders. The Christian community in a secular society urgently needs leaders who are prepared for battle much more than for caretaking. This will always mean that leadership is vital for the Church to maintain momentum and inspiration. A brief example of how St Paul led the community would be helpful here.

As a person, Paul was very gifted and yet very limited. The situation in his day was not all that different from today. Paul not only challenges modern leadership but also encourages it. Paul became the focal point and spearhead of the early community's surge into a pagan society. *Commitment* is the greatest attribute we can give to Paul. He is a leader who is relevant to society. He finds his authority in the Lord and from the other twelve apostles. He is grounded in the unity of the Church. He sees himself as a servant. He is able to live with and deal with diversity. He is versatile and resilient and does not compromise the truth of the Gospels.

Paul is community-orientated, and has the ability to work with a variety of groups, all of whom have different problems and needs. He shows a deep empathy and affirms communities while at the same time he exhorts and challenges them. He does not walk away from confrontation, but clarifies and addresses the problems in a creative way. He encourages participation in the community and does not hold on to power. We see him creating new leaders in situ and prepared to delegate. He speaks into a pagan world and is prepared to debate and elucidate. However, at the end of the day, the preoccupation with Paul is to build community using differing techniques to do so. Paul is a powerful example of someone who is struck by the unresolved tension between individualism and community and clearly pitches his tent firmly in the community camp.

Leaders can be dynamic, natural and well-trained. They may even be extremely charismatic and attractive for others to follow, but if their lifestyle is not in accordance with good living then it will all fall apart and the community will suffer. No one is free from sin yet there is an expectancy among those who follow that leaders in whom they trust should be moral, honest and just. In building community, it is so necessary to have good leadership lifestyle. 'The way a . . . leader operates, no matter what the cultural expectation, must be compatible with the moral demands . . . and consistent with [ethical living].'[14]

Call to Politicians

Tony Blair, the leader of the British Labour Party, wrote in 1993:

> Central to Christianity is the belief in equality; not that we are uniform in character or position, but on the contrary that despite our differences we are entitled to be treated equally . . . above all it is about the union between the individual and community. This philosophy is . . . used . . . to distinguish it from selfishness or even individualism.[15]

Human life is always and everywhere carried on in community of some sort. If this were not so then human life would cease. Community has taken differing forms. There are, however, certain characteristics which any human community must possess if it is to be a real form of community. It must be a group of people living together on certain terms which are public and known to all of them. This will define the stature of membership and enable each member to know what is expected of them and in turn what they are to expect. This will give the community a definite structure and a corporate identity.

Politicians should have a practical concern for the wellbeing of all citizens. There can be no 'real' nation where politics is indifferent to the lot of any of its citizens. This is seen at its best when politicians see to it that citizens get enough money to provide for their material needs. People need food, clothing and shelter to keep them alive. The most basic right, therefore, is the right to work.

> The man who presses for 'equality of opportunity' is urging that certain factors like wealth, which has hitherto determined the extent of an individual's opportunities, should be neutralised.[16]

There has been a rise in the Western world of the 'new right movement'. This is seeking to appease the individual and will only serve to swing nations into a new era of selfish individualism. 'Privatise' is the language of greed and individualism. It is certainly not the language of community. What 'privatise' means in practice is that the owners of utilities get as much profit as they can, but inevitably this is at the expense of the less well-off. This closes the markets by individualism and causes unemployment in the area of low-paid jobs. We must pay wages sufficient for earner and family. In most Western countries at the moment we see cuts. These cuts are usually not aimed at the very wealthy but at the 'lower' classes. They normally revolve around health and education. No politician in their right mind should ever attempt to cut these two vital areas of community life. Our young people – faced with 'dole queues', bad housing, bad education, bad health care – will become disenchanted and even dysfunctional.

There is emerging a new underclass of people in Western

culture: the unemployed, the broken family and the disenchanted youth. These are sometimes portrayed as lazy, unemployable, 'lager louts', and drug abusers or pushers. Is it possible that the rise of individualism in politics is enhancing some of these conditions and politically moving the so-called 'goal posts' away from community? Is it not true that people reared in socially and economically deprived areas are forced into low wage jobs and social deprivation?

The politician needs to hear again the call of community and not just the call of the rich and privileged within it. The call of those who desire greater wealth in things like privatised companies is no greater than the call of the little old lady living alone whose vote is forgotten. It is only when politicians listen to the voices of the marginalised that the nation as community will begin to grow.

I realise that not all members of society are committed to the principles of community or indeed social responsibility. There is no reason why politicians need to lose the high idealism of community and the practical considerations of endeavouring to meet the needs of all. Politicians must lay aside human aspirations for personal wealth and achievement so that the common political good can be served. I call politicians to exercise their duty in what I describe as the 'sacrament of politics'. I call it so because politicians have in their hands the lives of people, especially the voiceless. It is imperative, therefore, that politics never loses sight of community building. The politician who looks after the poor, old, lonely, sick, infirm and handicapped may never be popular in their own lifetime. Nevertheless, the immoral politics of individualism will inevitably become bankrupt as it compromises community usually for wealth and power.

At the same time because of the dignity of the human person the individual has rights and duties that are universal and inviolable. Every human being should have ready access to ... food, clothes, housing, education, work, respect and the right to act according to a correct conscience.[17]

Call for Ecology

There are advances today in transport, communications, materials, agriculture, nutrition and medicine. Yet with the advance in all of these also come dangers. Increasingly, people are conscious of the problems of pollution, for example. This is partly attributed to the advancements we have made, accompanied by the fear of what we can do to the earth. None of the evils attributed to modern science can be compared with the ultimate tragedy of a nuclear holocaust upon the human race and upon the earth.

Nature was not put on our planet for us to exploit, but rather that we should be good stewards of created matter. If, then, we acknowledge one unity we can more easily attempt to be ecological. The development of species depends upon a large variety of factors including climate, light, the availability of soil and water. These and more will determine the diversity and productivity of created matter.

Likewise community in the ecological sense ... includes all of the population of a given area. The community and the non-living environment function together as an ecological system or ecosystem.[18]

The first step that we must take as people united with nature is to reject the idea of humans as conquerors of nature. We are not licensed to kill or to become God's pest upon earth. A call to repentance is needed for the damage we have already done. We are not above ecological laws. It is necessary for all of us not just to challenge individuals but also institutions which pollute and abuse the unity of nature.

Second, education is vital in relation to science in general but to environmental science in particular. Polluters of all kinds have been experts at deceiving the general public in ecological matters, particularly where large sums of money are concerned. It is necessary to utilise the media correctly so that people can be informed of the true nature of abuse being executed upon the environment. Public opinion needs to be harnessed so that further pollution and exploitation can be avoided. This will then go a long way to developing a human conservation movement independent of committees and fringe organisations. The efforts of ecologists and conservationists must be directed to creating and channelling the necessary information to enable the media to get it right. This will also necessitate a dependence on the scientific world in obtaining the correct information. In this way scientists and technologists will enable the communicators to make a full audit of the situation and thereby create an accurate picture for us 'lay people'.

Third, planning teams need to be put in place to see that industry adheres to correct codes of operation. Most industries have gone to great lengths to ensure that the earth is left safe from things like pollution, yet a few have slipped through the net. These make demands upon air and water. Sometimes ecology and conservation are relatively less important than the production of jobs and wealth.

Evidently what is needed is more realistic assessment of what is meant by living standards and the quality of life. You do not have to be rich to be healthy and happy.[19]

One thing is sure: we need to get 'right' the idea that there is a relationship between humankind and our world. Our wellbeing matters to the extent that we need to understand and co-operate with the relationship between the two. Environmentalism is so important because of this interaction between the human and the natural. This will enrich our vision of community and stop us abusing selfishly the resources of our earth.

Conclusion – The Unresolved Tension

This book is about community and individualism – the unresolved tension. Some of us have to accept our own essential solitude; yet without community we drift down the road of individualism that leads to alienation and isolation. However, there is a widespread feeling that the promises of the modern era are slipping away from us. The modern-day attitudes of enlightenment and liberation have freed us from the bonds of faith, Church, family institution and all kinds of so-called 'oppression'; yet we are left lonely and alone. Sciences which were to have unlocked the realm of nature have given us the power to destroy it. 'Progress', in the language of today, seems to be leading us into the abyss. The sin of individualism that we saw originating from the primal family of Adam and Eve is being acted out on the stage of life. We do not seem to have learned the lesson that 'together' we 'get it together'.

Yet despite the analysis which I have made of a divided and separate world and Church there is still great optimism within me. I walk in hope. I realise that though the processes of separation and individualisation are present, there is a new mood to balance them by a commitment to community. This renewal is necessary and evident so that a new birth can be given to the world and the Church. Modernity may well be the culture of separation, yet within the fragments of our being there is still the wish to belong; a desire to belong to God, aspirations to belong to Church (community), and the knowledge that we belong to the world. There is a Godly discontent with this situation.

We in the Church are in a delightful situation in that we have the faith, background and ability to be prophetic to the world in leading it towards community. There are still great traditions around us to tell us about the nature of God, the nature of the world, the nature of society and who we are as people. We still have the voices that proclaim where our origin lies and where our destiny is calling us. The communities that already exist and the new ones that are emerging continue to give us the meaning of living life together and the dignity of each person. Many of our religious communities recognise the importance of community and are endeavouring to update; even in the secular world we are recognising the importance of family.

In short, we are not just a bunch of individuals moving into the abyss of isolation where we have very little in common. The voice of community needs to proclaim the difference that community can make in transmitting a qualitative distinctiveness in living. We owe the meaning of community to God the Trinity. This understanding of community will haunt us and constantly disturb us to seek and find new ways of belonging to each other. We search for 'smallness' where we can be known, loved, appreciated and open. Modernity and post-modernity have tried to obliterate the culture of community but they cannot erase it from our memory because at the end of the day the calling to unity and community is the domain of God himself. It is a call to integration and belonging to him and each other.

I base my hope upon the thousands of youth that I meet each year. There is a restlessness among them and a stirring that goes beyond individualism. They see that we can no longer view the world and its peoples in terms of compartments or boundaries. They recognise that we cannot have a 'separatist' mentality. They search for a Utopia; after all isn't that our origin? We as the Church need to capitalise on this search. We need to be living examples of community, where integration with God is seen and healing is offered. We need visibly to show the poverty of individualism in our holistic community lifestyles.

> The Church no longer has the luxury of being able to wait for centuries or even decades . . . It is time for courageous leadership . . . to create the new out of the old.[1]

All of these things give us new hope as we try to live the 'unresolved tension'.

Notes

Chapter 1. A Community of Three

1. Josiah Royce, *The Problem of Christianity*, Chicago University Press, 1968, pp. 75–98.
2. J. Moltmann, *History and the Triune God*, SCM Press, 1991, p. 126ff.
3. *The Private Life of Plants*, BBC TV, 1995.
4. J. Denzinger, *Enchiridion Symbolorum*, 26th edn, Frieburg, 1947.
5. John McKenzie, *Dictionary of the Bible*, Geoffrey Chapman, 1968, pp. 899–900.
6. W. Pannenberg, *The Apostles' Creed*, SCM Press, 1972, pp. 61–70.
7. Paul Leslie, *Son of Man*, Hodder and Stoughton, 1961, p. 174.
8. Pannenberg, *The Apostles' Creed*, pp. 36–7.
9. Thomas Aquinas, *Summa Theologiae*, 1 q 26 a.1.
10. David Pimm, *Speaking Mathematically*, Routledge and Kegan Paul, 1987, pp. 1–21.
11. Fred Milson, *His Leadership and Ours*, Epworth Press, 1969, pp. 24–5.
12. R. Eckardt, ed., *The Theologian at Work*, SCM Press, 1968, p. 34.
13. John Bowen, *Edward Schillebeeckx*, SCM Press, 1983, p. 42.
14. Walter Kasper, *Theology and the Church*, SCM Press, 1989, p. 105.
15. James Mackey, *The Christian Experience of God as Trinity*, SCM Press, 1983, p. 7.
16. Walter Kaufmann, *Nietzsche*, Meridian Books, 1950, p. 81.
17. Paul Schilpp, ed., *The Philosophy of Bertrand Russell*, Tutor

Publishing Company, 1951, p. 546.

18. George Carey, *I Believe in Man*, Hodder and Stoughton, 1977, p. 161.
19. Leonardo Boff, *Trinity and Society*, trans. Paul Burns, Burns and Oates, 1988, p. 3.
20. Boff, *Trinity and Society*, p. 16.

Chapter 2. The Community of Original Blessings

1. Colin Humphrey, *Creation and Evolution*, Oxford University Press, 1985.
2. Brenda Lehman and Edward Robinson, *The Mystery of Creation*, Christian Education Movement, 1983, p.3.
3. Günther Bornkamm, *Jesus of Nazareth*, Hodder and Stoughton, 1960, p. 119.
4. Thomas Merton, *Conjectures of a Guilty Bystander*, Sheldon Press, 1977, p. 217.
5. Hugh Montefiore, ed., *Man and Nature*, Collins, 1975. p. 27.
6. Ken Wilber, *Up From Eden*, Routledge and Kegan Paul, 1983, pp. 1–11.
7. Letty Russell, *Becoming Human*, Westminster Press, 1982. p. 22.
8. William Hamilton, *The Essence of Christianity*, Darton, Longman and Todd, 1961, p. 114.
9. Dorothee Solle, *Thinking About God*, SCM Press, 1991, pp. 42–52.
10. D. F. Owens, *What is Ecology?*, Oxford University Press, 1980, p. 2.
11. John Black, *The Dominion of Man*, Edinburgh Press, 1970, pp. 56–7.
12. R. S. Lee, *Freud and Christianity*, Penguin, 1948, p. 23.
13. J. McDavid and H. Harari, *Psychology and Social Behaviour*, Harper and Row, 1968, p. 238.

Chapter 3. A Covenant Community

1. Anthony Hoekema, *Created in God's Image*, Paternoster, 1986, pp. 140–1.
2. Stanley Chesnut, *The Old Testament Understanding of God*, Westminster Press, 1968, p. 50.

3. G. Anderson and T. Stransky, eds, *Mission Trends No. 2*, Paulist Press, 1975, p. 24.

4. George Hillery Jn., *Communal Organisations*, University of Chicago Press, 1968, p. 1.

5. Robert Davidson, *The Old Testament*, Hodder and Stoughton, 1964, pp. 45–6.

6. H. Cunliffe-Jones, *Jeremiah*, SCM Press, 1960, pp. 32, 198.

7. Alan Bryman, *Leadership and Organisations*, Routledge and Kegan Paul, 1986, p. 3.

8. L. Perdue and B. Kovacs, eds., *A Prophet to the Nations*, Eisenbrauns Publishing, 1984, pp. 151–61.

9. L. Perdue and B. Kovacs, *A Prophet to the Nations*, p. 367.

10. B. S. Childs, *Exodus*, SCM Press, 1974, pp. 397–8.

11. Mark L. Y. Chan, ed., *Mercy Community and Ministry*, Catalyst Books, 1993, p. 17.

12. *New Wine* magazine, February 1980, p. 30.

13. J. Mays and P. Achtemeier, eds, *Interpreting the Prophets*, Fortress Press, 1987, p. 200.

14. John Bright, *Covenant and Promise*, SCM Press, 1977, p. 44.

15. J. Moltmann, *The Experiment Hope*, SCM Press, 1975, p. 35.

Chapter 4. Jesus and Community

1. Pat Lynch, *'Awakening the Giant,'* Darton, Longman and Todd, 1990.

2. E. F. Schumacher, *Small is Beautiful*, Blond and Briggs, 1973.

3. F. Sontay, *How Philosophy Shapes Theology*, Harper and Row, 1971, pp. 357–82.

4. M. E. Shaw, *Group Dynamics*, McGraw-Hill, 1971, p. 5.

5. S. Sandmel, *A Jewish Understanding of the New Testament*, SPCK, pp. 18–31.

6. Lynch, *Awakening the Giant*, p. 62.

7. M. Preston-Shoot, *Effective Groupwork*, Macmillan, 1987 pp. 14–15.

8. Howard Snyder, *Liberating the Church*, Marshalls, 1983, pp. 114, 116.

9. Dietrich Bonhoeffer, *The Cost of Discipleship*, SCM Press, 1959, p. 36.

10. Rudolf Dreikurs, *Psychology of the Classroom*, Harper and Row, 1957, p. 87.
11. E. Gibbs, *Followed or Pushed*, Marc Europe, 1987, p. 115.
12. Helen Doohan, *Leadership in Paul*, Michael Glazier Inc., Delaware, 1984, p. 24.

Chapter 5. The Fledgling Communities

1. F. F. Bruce, *The Book of Acts*, Marshall, Morgan and Scott, 1965, p. 47.
2. A. S. Herbert, *The Book of the Prophet Isaiah 40–46,* Cambridge University Press, 1975, pp. 160–4.
3. R. R. Williams, *The Acts of the Apostles*, SCM Press, 1959, p. 49.
4. F. F. Bruce, *The Spreading Flame*, Paternoster, 1958, p. 74.
5. Joseph Martos, *Doors to the Sacred*, SCM Press, 1966, p. 239.
6. William Maxwell, *An Outline of Christian Worship*, Oxford University Press, 1960, p. 3.
7. R. Martin, *The Spirit and the Congregation*, Eerdmans, 1984, p. 2.
8. M. Amis, *Success*, Jonathan Cape, 1978, cover page.
9. *The Bible Designed to be Read as Literature*, Heinemann, p. 1047.
10. Bruce, *The Book of Acts*, p. 108.
11. J. McMannus, Ed, *The Oxford Illustrated History of Christianity*, Oxford University Press, 1990, pp. 21–8.
12. Richard Harries, *Is there a Gospel for the Rich?* Mowbrays, 1992, p. 32.
13. J. Dunn, *Baptism in the Spirit*, SCM Press, 1970, pp. 23–37.

Chapter 6. The Pilgrims of Community

1. Morley Rattenbury, *A Sketch of Church History*, Epworth Press, 1962, pp. 11–22.
2. Clement of Rome, *Epistle to the Corinthians*. This was written about the year 90 AD.
3. Tertullian, *Apology*, in *Fathers of the Church*, pp. 99–100.
4. *The Churches Separated from Rome*, A. Matthews, trans., Latourette, 1907.
5. B. Ward, ed., *Sayings of the Desert Fathers*, Mowbrays, 1975, p. 5.
6. 'Corpus Scriptorum Ecclesiasticorum Latinonorum 32 II', St

Ambrose of Milan, *De Nabuthae*, C. Schenkl, ed., 1847, pp. 460–70.

7. A. Way, ed., *Basil Letters*, No. 223 in *Fathers of the Church*, Washington DC 1955.

8. Sozomenus, *A History of the Church*, Bagsters, 1846, pp. 305–6.

9. P. Schrotenboer, ed., *Roman Catholicism*, Baker Book House, 1987, pp. 75–83.

10. L. Gilkey, *Catholicism Confronts Modernity*, Seabury Press, 1975, pp. 128–55.

11. *The Church in the Modern World*, Vatican II, No. 40; also *National Conference of Priests (England and Wales) Newspaper*. No. 31, October 1995.

12. O. Chadwick, *The Mind of the Oxford Movement*, Adam and Charles Black, 1960, p. 34.

13. G. Bennett, *To the Church of England*, Churchman Publishing, 1988, p. 135.

14. Faith Lees and Jeanne Hinton, *Love Is Our Home*, Hodder and Stoughton, 1978, p. 8.

15. David Watson, *I Believe in the Church*, Hodder and Stoughton, 1978, pp. 82–3.

16. D. Clarke, *Basic Communities*, SPCK, 1977; D. Clarke, *The Liberation of the Church*, Collins Fount, 1984; D. Clarke, *Yes to Life: In Search of the Kingdom Community*, Collins, Fount, 1987.

Chapter 7. Community–Protestant and Catholic

1. L. Newbigin, *The Household of God*, SCM Press, 1957, p. 103.

2. The term 'magisterial Reformation' refers to those Reformers who aligned themselves with civic authorities which co-operated in their programme of reform; for instance, Luther with the German princes, Zwingli with the city council in Zurich, Bucer with Strasbourg and Calvin with Geneva The term 'radical Reformation' refers to those who are also sometimes called 'Anabaptists', more extreme than the mainstream Reformers, condemning not only the Church of Rome but also all civil authority.

3. Alister E. McGrath, *A Life of John Calvin*, Blackwell, 1990, p. 182; Alister E. McGrath, *Evangelicalism and the Future of*

Christianity, Hodder and Stoughton, 1994, pp. 183–4; Dermot E. Fenlon, *Heresy and Obedience in Tridentine Italy*, Cambridge University Press, 1972.

4. *Dei Verbum* (Decree on Divine Revelation), Vatican II n. 21.
5. J. I. Packer, *Fundamentalism*, Eerdmans, 1958, p. 174.
6. Geoffrey Chapman, 1994, *Catechism of the Catholic Church*, sections 775–6.
7. Richard P. McBrien, *Catholicism*, Harper, 1981, p. 1180–3.
8. Richard Lints, *The Fabric of Theology: A Prolegomenon to Evangelical Theology*, Eerdmans, 1993, p. 83.
9. McBrien, *Catholicism*.
10. H. R. Trevor-Roper, *Religion, The Reformation and Social Change*, Macmillan, 1967, pp. 1–45.
11. Jacob Burckhardt, *The Civilization of the Renaissance in Italy*, New York, 1935, p. 143.
12. Peter Matheson, *Contarini at Regensburg*, Oxford University Press, 1972; Alister E. McGrath, *Iustitia Dei*, Cambridge University Press, 1986, vol. 2, section 25.
13. Scott H. Hendrix, *Luther and the Papacy: Stages in a Reformation Conflict*, Philadelphia, 1981 (cited in A. E. McGrath, *Reformation Thought*, Blackwell, 1993, second edn, p. 189).
14. W. P. Stephens, *The Theology of Huldrych Zwingli*, Oxford University Press, 1986.
15. John Calvin, *Institutes of the Christian Religion*, 1559, IV. i. 4.
16. Alister E. McGrath, *A Life of John Calvin*, Blackwell, 1990, pp. 188–90.
17. Finding their basis in Augustine's interpretation of the parable of the wheat and the tares (Matt. 13: 24–30) the Reformers held there to be a dialectic between the visible and invisible Church. The visible Church was the Church as we see it, 'mixed', consisting of both regenerate and unregenerate. The invisible Church was the eschatological Church, known only to God and to be finally revealed to all on the last day. Believers, however, could be assured of their being in the invisible as well as the visible Church.
18. Louis Bouyer, *Introduction to Spirituality*, Desclee Co., 1961, p. 11. See also his *Orthodox Spirituality and Protestant and Anglican Spirituality*, Burns and Oates, 1969.

19. *Lumen Gentium*, (Dogmatic Constitution on the Church), Vatican II n. 11.
20. *Lumen Gentium*, n. 8.
21. David Watson, *I Believe in the Church*, Hodder and Stoughton, 1978, p. 82–3.
22. Lesslie Newbigin, *The Gospel in a Pluralist Society*, SPCK, 1989; Lesslie Newbigin, *Foolishness to the Greeks*, SPCK, 1986; Lesslie Newbigin, *The Other Side of 1984*, WCC, Geneva, 1983.
23. P. Speed, *Social Problems of the Industrial Revolution*, Pergammon, 1975.
24. John Finney, *Finding Faith Today*, British and Foreign Bible Society, 1992.
25. Finney, *Finding Faith Today*, pp. 36–50.
26. Finney, *Finding Faith Today*, pp. 24–5.
27. *Christifideles Laici*, (The Vocation and The Mission of the Lay Faithful in the Church and in the World), John Paul II, 1988, n. 3.
28. Alister E. McGrath, *A Life of John Calvin*, Blackwell, 1990, pp. 234–6.
29. B. Meeking and J. Stott, eds, *The Evangelical/Roman Catholic Dialogue on Mission 1977–1984*, Paternoster, 1986.

Chapter 8. The Yearning of a Secular Society

1. Cf. Lesslie Newbigin, *The Gospel in a Pluralist Society*, SPCK, 1989, p. 111.
2. J. Collins, *Uncommon Cultures*, Routledge, 1989, p. 3.
3. C. Gunton, *The One, the Three and the Many*, Cambridge University Press, 1993, p. 18.
4. H. Garland and R. Grimsley, *The Age of Enlightenment*, Penguin, 1979, p. 9.
5. Jacob Burckhardt, *The Civilization of the Renaissance in Italy*, New York, 1935, p. 143.
6. Max Weber, *The Protestant Ethic and the Spirit of Capitalism*, translated by Talcott Parsons, Allen & Unwin, 1985.
7. Alister E. McGrath, *A Life of John Calvin*, Blackwell, 1990, pp. 219–45.
8. McGrath, *A Life of John Calvin*, p. 244.
9. Alasdair MacIntyre, *Marxism and Christianity*, Duckworth,

1995.
10. C. Gunton, *The One, the Three and the Many*, Cambridge University Press, 1993, p. 39.
11. Ibid., p. 214.
12. John D. Zizioulas, *Being as Communion: Studies in Personhood and the Church*, Darton, Longman and Todd, 1985.

Chapter 9. Church – Cult – Community

1. David Edwards, *Religion and Change*, Hodder and Stoughton, 1969, p. 236.
2. R. Niebuhr, *The Social Sources of Denominationalism*, Holts, New York, 1929, p. 19.
3. E. Heftmann, *Dark Side of the Moonies*, Penguin, 1982, p. 240.
4. T. Robbins, *Cults, Converts and Charisma*, Sage Publications, 1988, pp. 69–70.
5. E. T. Clarke, *Small Sects in America*, Abingdon Press, New York, 1937, p. 225.
6. Philip Hammond, ed., *The Sacred in a Secular Age*, University of California Press, 1985, p. 21.
7. R. Cialdini, *Influence: Science and Practice*, Scott Foresman and Co., 1985, p. 98.
8. S. Freud, *Group Psychology and the Analysis of the Ego*, The Hogarth Press, vol. 18, pp. 120–4.
9. J. Beckford, *Cult Controversies*, Tavistock, 1985, pp. 197–8.
10. R. Kanter, *Commitment and Community: Communes and Utopias in Sociological Perspective*, Harvard University Press, 1972, p. 88.
11. S. Harrison, *Cults*, Christopher Helm, 1990, pp. 6–24.
12. M. Galanter, *Cults*, Oxford University Press, 1989, p. 13.
13. *World in Action*, ITV television programme, 23 October 1995.
14. Harrison, *Cults*.
15. R. Stark and W. Bainbridge, *The Future of Religion*, University of California Press, 1985, pp. 126–48.
16. Documents of Vatican II: *The Church in the Modern World, Evangelisation of Peoples*, Pope Paul VI n. 13; 15; 18; 20.
17. Beckford, *Cult Controversies*, p. 155.
18. A. Deikman, *The Wrong Way*, Beacon Press, 1994, p. 173.

Chapter 10. Community Builders

1. A. Von Harnack, *Das Wesen Des Christentums*.
2. K. Hylson-Smith, *Evangelical in the Church of England*, T. and T. Clarke, 1988, p. 312.
3. George Marsden, *The Evangelical Mind and The New School Presbyterian Experience*, Yale University Press, 1970, p. 32.
4. Paul Schrotenboer, ed., *Roman Catholics*, Baker Book House, 1987, p. 64.
5. Ronald Sider, ed., *Lifestyle of the Eighties: And Evangelical Commitment to Simple Lifestyle*, Paternoster, 1982, pp. 131–2.
6. R. J. Neuhaus, *The Naked Public Square*, Eerdmans, 1984, p. 60.
7. A. Dumas, *Political Theology and the Life of the Church*, SCM Press, 1977, p. 23.
8. J. Dominian, *Christian Marriage*, Darton, Longman and Todd, 1967, p. 17.
9. *Decree on the Laity*, Vatican II, n. 11.
10. F. Robertson Elliot, *The Family Change on Continuity*, Macmillan, 1986, p. 5.
11. Richard Ellis, *Health in Childhood*, Penguin, 1960, p. 28.
12. Francis Moloney, *Disciples and Prophets*, Darton, Longman and Todd, 1982, p. 80.
13. Pope Paul VI, *Evangelica Testificatio*.
14. E. Gibbs, *Followed or Pushed*, MARC Europe, 1987, p. 86.
15. Christopher Bryant, ed., *Reclaiming the Ground*, Spire Books, 1993, p. 10.
16. S. I. Benn and R. S. Peters, *Social Principles and the Democratic State*, George Allen and Unwin, 1959, p. 120.
17. C. McOustra, *Love in the Economy*, St Paul's Publications, 1990, p. 71.
18. E. Odum, *Ecology*, University of Georgia Press, 1966, pp. 3–4.
19. D. F. Owen, *What is Ecology?* Oxford University Press, 1980, p. 205.

Conclusion

1. G. Moran and M. Harris, *Experiences in Community*, Burns and Oates, 1969, p. 205.